The Co-Teaching Power Zone

Navigating co-teacher power balances can be tricky. This refreshing book provides a new way to experience meaningful co-teaching collaborations by illuminating the value of working independently and then reconnecting in order to strengthen relationships and outcomes. Author Elizabeth Stein introduces the Co-Teaching Power Zone Framework, which includes a process of valuable disconnected co-teaching opportunities as well as the use of cogenerative dialogues, to help you cultivate a relationship that flows into the classroom environment and into daily instructional decisions. Each chapter includes example scenarios and reflection questions to help you apply the ideas to your own setting. With this book's realistic and helpful framework, you'll be able to transform your co-teaching practices while co-creating a culture of belonging with one another and with every learner in the room.

Elizabeth Stein has more than 30 years teaching experience as an educator, instructional coach, and educational consultant in grades K-12, specializing in universal design for learning (UDL) and special education. She teaches higher education courses on inclusive practices. Elizabeth is the author of multiple books on creating equitable and meaningful learning environments.

Other Eye On Education Books

Available from Routledge
(www.routledge.com/eyeoneducation)

Two Teachers in the Room
Strategies for Co-Teaching Success
Elizabeth Stein

The Co-Teacher's Guide
Intensifying Instruction Beyond One Teach, One Support
Jennifer L. Goeke

Shaking Up Special Education
Instructional Moves to Increase Achievement
Savanna Flakes

Specially Designed Instruction
Increasing Success for Students with Disabilities
Anne M. Beninghof

The Co-Teaching Power Zone
A Framework for Effective Relationships and Instruction

Elizabeth Stein

NEW YORK AND LONDON

First published 2024
by Routledge
605 Third Avenue, New York, NY 10158

and by Routledge
4 Park Square, Milton Park, Abingdon, Oxon, OX14 4RN

Routledge is an imprint of the Taylor & Francis Group, an informa business

© 2024 Taylor & Francis

The right of Elizabeth Stein to be identified as author of this work has been asserted in accordance with sections 77 and 78 of the Copyright, Designs and Patents Act 1988.

All rights reserved. No part of this book may be reprinted or reproduced or utilised in any form or by any electronic, mechanical, or other means, now known or hereafter invented, including photocopying and recording, or in any information storage or retrieval system, without permission in writing from the publishers.

Trademark notice: Product or corporate names may be trademarks or registered trademarks, and are used only for identification and explanation without intent to infringe.

ISBN: 9781032367712 (hbk)
ISBN: 9781032365466 (pbk)
ISBN: 9781003333692 (ebk)

DOI: 10.4324/9781003333692

Typeset in Palatino
by codeMantra

Contents

Meet the Author vii

Introduction. 1

PART I
Being: The Motivation Zone. 13

1 Connecting with the Co-teaching Power Zone. 15

2 Entering the Motivation Zone 23

3 Using the Conscious Co-teacher Action Planner 38

PART II
Belonging: The Collaboration Zone .43

4 Ramping Up Collaboration
   by Connecting, Disconnecting, and Reconnecting 45

5 Increasing Collaboration with the Co-teaching Models 56

PART III
Power: The Communication Zone. .67

6 Co-teaching in the Zone: Quick Check-in 69

7 Incorporating Cogenerative Dialogues 72

8 Using Story in Story (SiS) Approach to Expand
   Collaboration. 86

9 Tapping into Our Co-teaching Power with
   Discussion Tools...................................95

10 Implementing Impactful Instructional
    Approaches for Co-teaching Power 115

11 Applying Evidence-Based Practices within the
    Co-teaching Power Zone...........................134

   *Next Steps in Creating YOUR Co-teaching Power Zone
   Experiences*.. 150
   References 155

Meet the Author

Elizabeth Stein, Ed.D., has more than 30 years teaching experience including grades K-12, specializing in universal design for learning (UDL) and special education. She is currently an adjunct professor at Stony Brook University, New York, teaching principles and practices of inclusive education and a special education/UDL instructional coach and consultant. Elizabeth is National Board Certified in Literacy, and the author of *Elevating Co-Teaching through UDL* (CAST, 2016), *Elevating Co-Teaching with Universal Design for Learning: Revised and Expanded Edition* (CAST, 2023), *Two Teachers in the Room: Strategies for Co-Teaching Success* (Routledge, 2017), and other publications.

Introduction

Co-teachers all over share a story of solidarity. We are all connected through many stories of effective and many (far too many) stories of unbalanced, inequitable co-teaching practices. In solidarity, we know we are not alone when we experience common challenges. Examples of these challenges include:

1. Creating and sustaining **relationships**
2. Participating in **meaningful co-planning time**
3. **Engaging as an active participant** throughout all phases of instruction

My first co-teaching experience (over two decades ago!) ended up being a great success—but it didn't start out that way. The following years resulted in the wildest roller coaster ride imaginable. There were unpredictable highs and lows that resulted in a serious range of heart pounding and energy boosting trepidation with a balance of thrill-seeking joy. Through it all, I was always compelled to get back on the ride, buckle back up, and experience it—learn and grow with it—each day—year after year—come what may.

Thinking about the students was my driving force that fed my passion for co-teaching. They needed ME! They needed a co-teacher who would advocate for equitable learning environments and activate their abilities to learn alongside their same-aged peers in the general classroom. And boy, was I up for that!

At that early point in my co-teaching career (circa 2002), I was idealistic (and I still am, thankfully!). I thought that showing up to the classroom with the exuberance, passion, and pedagogical knowledge to co-teach would be met with open arms. I don't have to tell you what happened next—but let's review. Here's the part where you buckle up! The roller coaster ride really begins to take off here!

The reality of teaching with various co-teachers resulted in my own personal and professional growth. I co-taught in classrooms where I felt free to contribute my style, strategies, and voice. I also experienced the twists, flips, and flops of co-teaching in classrooms where I felt stunted and stifled. In those cases, I felt forced to adjust my actions leaving me in that all too familiar "helping teacher" role. My stomach drops just writing about it here! It was a visceral sensation of frustration and fear. Fear that I was not doing enough for the students. Frustration for how to make time to teach them the strategies they needed. Fear of what would happen if I spoke up for my role as a special educator—in the moments of class time. (Oh, the many sleepless nights I endured—as I planned for the next day with a solution-seeking mindset.)

Thankfully, there were many occasions where my co-teacher and I rolled through the ride with the thrill of embracing the ups and downs together. Clearly, the meaning of "co" makes all the difference. It saddens me to know that co-teaching remains such a challenging process for far too many—even after all these years. I am grateful to be at a point where I can take my experiences, research, actions, and interactions and offer a framework that guides and bolsters co-teachers to respond to the most common co-teaching challenges by living within the co-teaching power zone.

In general, when we are "in the zone" we feel empowered, we feel light on our feet, and downright giddy about doing the task at hand with great skill and gratitude. This is certainly true for many co-teachers who feel life is good! They appreciate working and learning alongside their teaching partner. Yet, far too often, co-teachers feel the challenges of communicating, co-planning, and co-teaching in the same room. This book expands the notion of being "in the zone" to include all variations of co-teaching scenarios. The co-teaching power zone welcomes all co-teaching realities from the familiar lackluster and disempowered to the highly engaged, committed, and enthusiastic co-teachers—and everyone in between. The zone welcomes YOU and meets every co-teacher and pairing where they are and supports them along the way to co-create the most effective co-teaching experience. Co-teaching, come what may (Stein, 2023).

Welcome to the co-teaching power zone where every co-teacher is valued—accepted—included—actively involved—and supported to engage in the natural process of being a learner—within the co-teaching relationship. Power is the focus because it influences any co-teaching relationship and directly impacts student learning. The zone promises that once entered, each co-teacher will have the opportunity to become more aware of how their relationship impacts their instruction and learning environment. The aim of the Co-teaching Power Zone (CPZ) Framework is to boost co-teaching consciousness with the aim of organically and authentically supporting every teacher toward the most meaningful and effective co-teaching experience with each unique pairing. It honors the individual within a much-needed partnership approach. Once more aware, oh, the co-teaching moves that can be made in co-powered progression. No need to wait any longer…let's begin with some theory that guides our understanding for our actions within the zone.

The Theories that Inform Effective Co-teaching Experiences in the Zone

As a collection, the theories create continuous flow of inward and outward movement with flexibility and freedom (Stein, 2021, p. 21). It mimics the natural process of interactions between co-teachers. Specifically, the theories explain how co-teachers may co-create a natural flow between their internal communication as they become more aware of their perspective and ideas. In addition, the theories help to explain the external interactions between co-teachers and students. An image of a willow tree's downward arching pendulant branches depicts the movement and free flow of intentional actions and how the theories organize, clarify, and guide co-teachers' interactions to create meaningful co-teaching experiences.

Through the lens of various evidence-based theories, co-teachers may begin to understand how their individual and collective actions contribute to the state of their co-teaching occurrences. They may rejoice in celebration, or they may find themselves understanding the gaps they need to fill, so they may become more effective co-teachers together. Let's take a look at the theories that feed into this interactive CPZ Framework. See Figure 0.1 Theories that Inform the CPZ Framework.

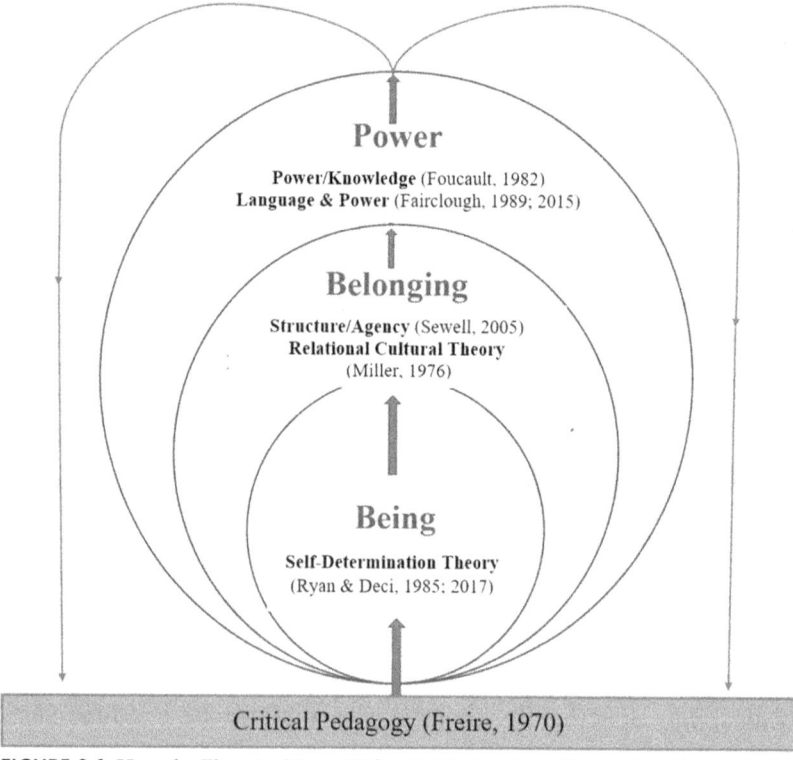

FIGURE 0.1 How the Theories Move Within the Co-teaching Power Zone Framework. (Adapted from Stein, 2021).

How to Use the Theories that Feed into CPZ Applications

Like the strong roots of a willow tree—nourished by sunlight and water—critical pedagogy serves as the foundation for understanding and applying the CPZ Framework. Key principles of critical pedagogy that feed into CPZ include:

- Engaging in **reciprocal, consistent, and transparent communication** in order to increase awareness (conscientization) and continue to learn as multiple perspectives are embraced.
- **Participating actively** throughout all phases of the learning process in order to experience a sense of freedom to think and to expand one's view by actively and critically thinking and learning with others.
- Empowering self and others through ongoing **reflection** in order to experience the momentum of learning and growing as one engages in a deeper level of thinking about their actions and the actions of those around them in order to keep improving.
- Through reflection and what we learn—both from the content—and from listening to
- Others' perceptions and perspectives, we have a chance to keep learning and improving. This **transformative process** allows us to remain learners while naturally improving our teaching practices.

Since co-teaching is a complex, nuanced process, critical pedagogy alone is not enough to create a framework to support and guide co-teachers. CPZ supports co-teachers' increased awareness in understanding their own views of their teaching styles, philosophy, and overall perspective on co-teaching and working with students of all abilities. This state of being with one's understanding in relationship with their perspective feeds into their willingness to understand the perspective of others—namely their co-teacher's perspective. This heightened awareness increases co-teachers' awareness by learning from and with the perspective of others.

Self-determination theory (SDT) explains what motivates a teacher to want to co-teach. We know the reality that some teachers are intrinsically motivated to co-teach. That is, they enjoy teaching alongside a colleague and sharing in the responsibilities and learning new ways of teaching and reaching students of varying abilities. While others must be forced into it through external pressures such as it is "their turn" or they are simply told they must do it. SDT feeds CPZ in a way that examines the environmental factors that facilitate or undermine one's willingness to co-teach. Through over 40 years of empirical evidence, SDT claims there are three universal needs that when met result in intrinsic motivation and overall wellness. The three basic needs have shown predictive and practical value that when met serve as effective intervention in everyday responsibilities (Ryan & Deci, 2017). CPZ upholds that when these basic needs are supported, better co-teaching outcomes are produced and result in higher quality and stronger motivated co-teachers who experience individual and collective wellness. Each co-teacher must have support in meeting the three basic needs of:

- ♦ **Autonomy**: Co-teachers are willing to co-teach and endorse one's own actions to be an active participant along every aspect of the co-teaching process.
- ♦ **Competence**: Co-teachers feel effective, capable, and engaged. They feel that they are contributing in meaningful ways.
- ♦ **Relatedness**: Co-teachers feel a sense of belonging within the teaching and learning environment. They feel that their perspective is valued and that they matter. They feel that they are able to optimally function as they contribute their personal expertise. They feel significant as they connect with their co-teacher and students.

Let's turn to how individual and collective co-teaching actions feed into classroom routines. According to Sewell and

Sewell (2005), the way individuals act becomes the structures and routines in place. Co-teachers provide the structures and routines of their class that determine the way their students will act. Similarly, the way one co-teacher acts inform the other co-teacher how to act. The relational cultural theory (Miller, 1976) feeds CPZ to explain how co-teachers must first and foremost consider how their actions influence the other as they remain open to mutual growth-fostering interactions. Each is willing to share and learn from and with each other. Of particular importance is the awareness that in order for a co-teaching relationship to be effective, co-teachers must make time to connect, disconnect, and reconnect through ongoing communication. The disconnection is of great importance as it allows time for each co-teacher to reflect and plan. The space between disconnection and reconnection is paramount. The only way co-teachers will reconnect is if their relationship experiences intentional moves in having their three basic needs (autonomy, competence, relatedness) met. This explains why too many co-teaching pairs do not work—they are simply not reconnecting—or connecting in the first place!

This sense of being and belonging feeds into an overall feeling of shared, connected power as co-teachers ultimately move toward challenging ableist views and value the knowledge and expertise that each co-teacher has to offer (Foucault, 1982). Within the CPZ Framework, we will also explain how the language we use is a form of power that has the opportunity to facilitate or undermine effective co-teaching experiences.

All theories will be expressed in very practical, manageable, and motivating ways throughout this book. It is my hope that the CPZ Framework provides you with the answers who have finally received when asking the question: *What is it that makes some co-teaching experiences work and others not?* Furthermore, let's consider CPZ as a solution to eliminating the externally regulated "it's your turn to co-teach" process and replacing it with well-supported intrinsically motivating co-teaching opportunities.

"We Are Like Two Pieces of a Puzzle"

Many of these theories guided me through my research as I worked with two co-teachers, Ms. D. and Ms. K. with the aim of studying their classroom culture, and the possible ways they co-created a sense of belonging with their students (Stein, 2021). On individual occasions, they each used the metaphor of two puzzle pieces. Ms. K. explained to me that they were "two puzzle pieces that fit perfectly together. Everybody, including the parents see it and tell us." In a separate individual conversation with me, Ms. D shared "We just clicked. We are two pieces to a puzzle, and we are on the same page and have similar values and teaching styles" (p. 83). It was clear that in addition to being comfortable with their own abilities as an educator, they were open to sharing their ideas and feelings with one another. Ms. D and Ms. K serve as a representation of an effective co-teaching pairing that may commonly stir up an image of two puzzle pieces that fit and click easily (Figure 0.2).

I extend this notion of two pieces of a puzzle that "just click" and fit so perfectly together to a more realistic view of the many other pieces involved in making two teacher "just click." I share a more comprehensive look at what may guide two puzzle pieces to fit together through the lens of a cyclical natural process of collaboration (see Figure 0.3). The foundation of the CPZ Framework guides two co-teachers piece together five active processes that allow the two pieces to fit in the first place.

FIGURE 0.2 We just click

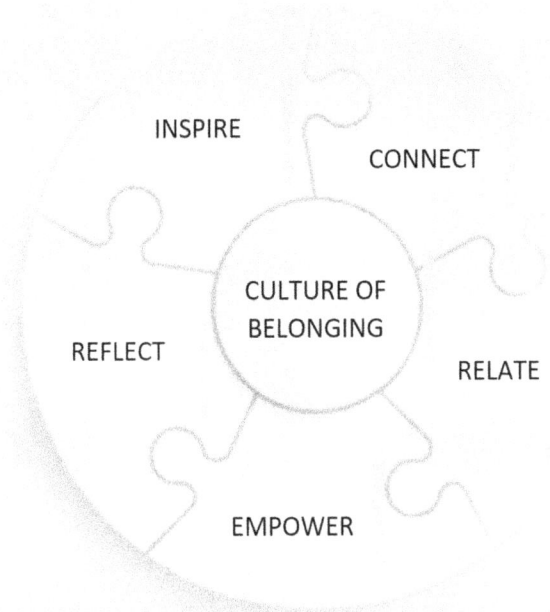

FIGURE 0.3 Five attributes of co-teaching within the CPZ Framework

This five-piece puzzle displays the evolving process two co-teachers are committed to as they follow the natural flow of the CPZ Framework. The circular formation of the completed puzzle symbolizes the ongoing development in co-creating a culture of belonging in any co-taught classroom. It is an ongoing commitment to being in a co-teaching relationship with a willingness to learn from and with one another. Let's take a quick look at the general focus of each puzzle piece toward co-creating meaningful and sustainable co-teaching relationships.

Inspire: What is your motivation to co-teach? What skills do you bring to the co-teaching experience? What is your co-teacher's motivation to co-teach? What skills do they bring to your co-teaching team?

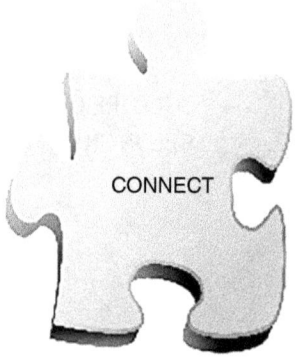

Connect: Pay attention to your inner voice—what are you telling yourself? How does your inner dialogue affect your actions and the way you connect with your co-teacher and students? How may you shift your inner thoughts to create actions that optimize your connection with your co-teacher? After each co-teacher reflects individually, communicate with reciprocity and transparency.

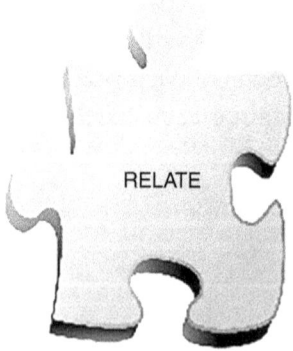

Relate: Connect with one another through a natural process of collaboration. The CPZ framework introduces the process of connecting, disconnecting, and reconnecting to engage in a growth-fostering relationship that optimizes the opportunity for transformative co-teaching experiences.

Empower: Each co-teacher becomes more aware of their individual strengths and areas for improvement. Together they apply their individual and collective abilities while learning from and with one another.

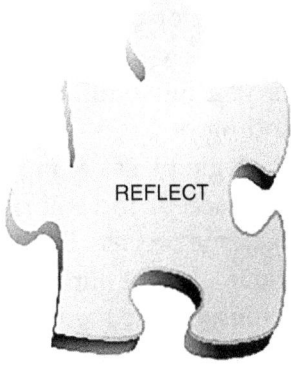

Reflect: Through a strong process of communication and collaboration, co-teachers experience an ongoing reflective process that empowers their ations and interactions.

How to Use This Book

This book is intended to be a self-paced personal professional learning experience between two co-teachers—with me right by your side along the way! I mean that literally. Co-teachers may use any one of the many ways to contact me to launch discussions that continue to improve co-teaching experiences (see the end of the book). The overall intention of the book is to introduce a framework that guides co-teachers to negotiate their individual and collective power as they create a relationship that effectively permeates through all phases of instruction and the learning environment. The book is segmented into three parts to guide the movement of an internal, personal connection that moves to external more collaborative actions. Each chapter builds upon the previous chapter, so those new to co-teaching will likely benefit from moving through the book sequentially. Once the CPZ Framework is understood, the book may be applied by seeking out activities that co-teachers feel they would benefit from most at that time. The overarching goal is to allow two co-teachers to embrace and negotiate their personal and collective power to allow for ongoing improvements as they learn with one another in authentic ways. This book presents an opportunity for you to be open to let the transformation happen—to improve your personal teaching skills as you learn from and with your co-teaching partner. As you move along through this book—and with your understanding of CPZ—you will earn puzzle pieces along the way. At strategic places along your reading, you will have the opportunity to accept and embrace where you are along the co-teaching power zone process. See the Afterword for puzzle piece template for you to use: cut out and hang in your classroom to build your co-teaching puzzle together through the year.

Now what are we waiting for? Let's get to it!

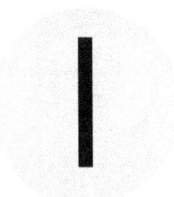

Being
The Motivation Zone

Chapter 1: Connecting with the Co-teaching Power Zone
Chapter 2: Entering the Motivation Zone
Chapter 3: Using the Conscious Co-teacher Action Planner

1
Connecting with the Co-teaching Power Zone

Mr. Fisher and Ms. Smith were immersed in the flow of learning with their students. Each teacher stopped to sit with groups of students. After ten minutes, Ms. Smith shared "What do you think Mr. Fisher—are we almost ready?"

"Yes, this side of the room is just about done!" responded Mr. Fisher.

Ms. Smith added, "This side, too!" Mr. Fisher and Ms. Smith went on to provide additional support to students who needed additional visuals or vocabulary and ideas clarified. They both noticed that many students were naturally supporting their peers in the learning process, simply by the materials the teachers prepared and the natural conversation in each group.

The students completed their conversations and group work. The teachers continued to check in with specific groups, and after three minutes both teachers gave each other a knowing nod. Mr. Fisher then directed the class back to the front board where he reviewed some key points of the lesson. Ms. Smith concluded the lesson by initiating a whole class conversation where each group shared how their work together connected with the key points that Mr. Fisher just reviewed. Both teachers engaged the students in an enriching class discussion. As the bell rang, one student's voice could be heard above the energizing dialogue. "I wish we could stay in this class all day!"

Welcome to co-teaching in the zone where Ms. Smith and Mr. Fisher present one example of how effective co-teaching relationships impact the instruction and overall learning environment. The way they communicated and shared responsibilities during all phases of class time optimized the opportunities for their students to feel a sense of belonging as they actively participated along with both teachers.

The co-teaching power zone (CPZ) honors each individual within a much-needed partnership approach. It honors the human condition. That is, the reality that being in teaching partnerships can be challenging. The CPZ Framework offers a readily accessible and contextual framework to meet every individual teacher and co-teaching pair where they as they are guided to personally experience their year of co-teaching practices together in transformative ways. The CPZ Framework provides a structured, yet flexible, pathway that supports moving within personal co-teaching experiences with grace—at all times—without exception—without judgment. It honors the entry point of individual co-teachers as they join together in partnership—while increasing and maintaining a strong connection with their individual strengths, skills, and hopes as a co-teacher. As teachers increase their awareness of their place within the CPZ, they have the opportunity to strengthen that spirited commitment to learning that improving that distinguishes the most effective co-teaching experiences possible. The CPZ dignifies the various ways in which each co-teacher brings a unique perspective to the teaching team. Each co-teacher leverages their personal beliefs, skills, and experiences through an ongoing collaborative process. This process illuminates the personal power of each co-teacher and the ways they may meaningfully contribute within their team. Imagine that! A world where each co-teacher has a sense of personal value and belonging within all phases of the co-teaching process. It's not too good to be true! It is called living in the CPZ.

Three Interconnected Experiences of the Co-teaching Power Zone

As co-teachers embrace co-teaching through the power zone framework, they become naturally a part of three interconnected and interactional experiences for working toward ongoing growth and transformative co-teaching practices in partnership. Being, belonging, and power address the layers of human need to make the most of any co-teaching process. The CPZ Framework offers a path, like a treasure map, toward creating consistent, sustainable, and effective co-teaching relationships that naturally impact the instructional process and overall learning environment. The ultimate goal is to co-create a culture of belonging in the classroom where every learner—including the two teachers—has the opportunity to feel competent, connected, and autonomous. The overarching commitment to co-teach within the power zone is the acknowledgment that each co-teaching relationship in the classroom serves as a catalyst that impacts instruction and the overall learning environment. For the most meaningful, personalized, and effective co-teaching to occur, each co-teacher must have a sense of belonging with one another first and foremost. The CPZ shares a few unique experiences.

1. Co-teachers have the opportunity to increase their self-awareness of their beliefs, values, and self-perceptions of co-teaching. This awareness grounds them in moving toward a collaborative partnership approach.
2. Collaboration is experienced through a natural and intentional process of connecting, disconnecting, and reconnecting. The CPZ embraces the process every co-teacher must disconnect to honor their individual power. Their power here is defined as a continual process of leveraging their personal strengths, learning preferences, skills, and experiences. Careful attention must be made to the timing of connecting and reconnecting following the need to disconnect. The reconnection allows for each

co-teacher to learn from and with one another. Without reconnection, co-teachers may easily fall into a dualistic approach that leaves one or both co-teachers feeling frustrated, overwhelmed, and isolated. The reconnection is what powers up the two co-teachers to join forces in partnership. The CPZ Framework makes this distinctive collaborative process visible by emphasizing mutuality and trust in observeable ways.

3. Dialogic tools are the way to illuminate and value every perspective. Each co-teacher has the opportunity to feel valued by sharing and empowered by listening and learning from their co-teacher's view. Dialogic tools include opportunities for individuals to express their thoughts, feelings, ideas, and overall perspective. The tools support cultivating the relationship that then naturally impacts the way they design and implement instruction and the culture in the classroom learning environment. Figure 1.1 illustrates the natural flow of the three interconnected experiences of the CPZ.

The interplay of these three natural human conditions frames and supports co-teachers to provide the structure that firmly roots them personally as they commit to co-teaching. Once individually rooted, they then can branch out and begin to use the

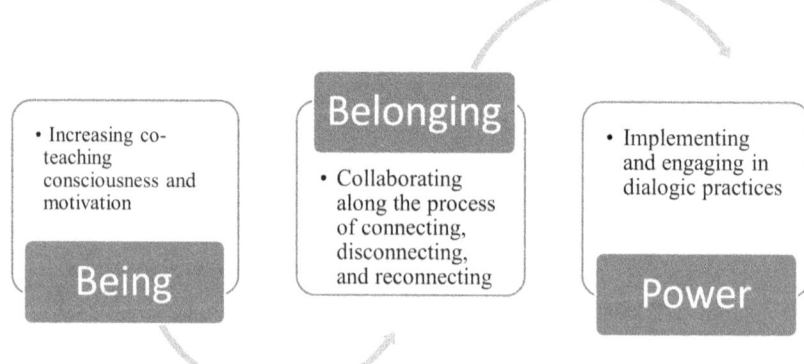

FIGURE 1.1 Illustrates the Natural Flow of the Three Interconnected Experiences of the Co-teaching Power Zone.

flexible structure of the framework to co-teach with freedom and effectiveness that honors every possible human response to co-teaching.

Being

The Motivation Zone provides a practical, relatable, and research-based entry point in creating co-teaching relationships. It describes three basic human needs and encourages each co-teacher to disconnect with one another to individually consider their personal stance as they enter and move along in their partnership. Embracing a sense of being is also supported through the idea of becoming a conscious co-teacher as each rooted educator begins to branch out to consider their co-teacher's view.

Belonging

The Collaboration Zone changes the way we currently think about co-teaching where it's all about connecting and joining together in partnership. The CPZ illuminates a process of connecting, disconnecting, and reconnecting as paramount in creating and sustaining the most effective co-teaching relationships. Individuals need to disconnect in order to value one another and to ensure that each individual is actively involved in every aspect of the co-teaching process. Additional emphasis here is on making mutuality and trust visible and observable, so that the reconnection happens in the most meaningful way to create two active teachers who feel competent, connected, and autonomous.

Power

The Communication Zone is where we can feel, experience, and observe the co-teaching like the pendulant branches of a willow tree. The freedom of motion by the trees branches is grounded by strong roots. Like the willow tree who is grounded by their roots, a co-teacher in the CPZ is grounded by the structure within the experiences of being and belonging. The freedom to co-teach within the CPZ Framework is supported by dialogic methods that support a strong communication process needed for any co-teaching experience. Examples of dialogic practices that will be provided include cogenerative dialogues, the story in story (SiS) approach (see Chapter 8…), as well as five instructional strategies that support dialogue in the classroom (see Chapter 10…..). For teachers to get the most out of teaching within the CPZ, there are five competencies that bolster their actions within the framework and specifically as they experience being, belonging, and power within their co-teaching world.

Key Takeaways

- ♦ The CPZ provides opportunities for honoring each co-teacher within a partnership approach.
- ♦ Each co-teacher has the opportunity to feel a sense of value and belonging from and with one another within all phases of the co-teaching process.
- ♦ The co-teaching relationship permeates through all phases of instruction and the overall learning environment.
- ♦ A unique process of collaboration within the CPZ includes two co-teachers who co-create a natural flow of connecting, disconnecting, and reconnecting to honor their individual and collective power.
- ♦ Being, belonging, and power are three interconnected experiences that provide co-teachers with the opportunities to increase their self-awareness, collaboration, and application of their personal and collective power through dialogue.

Co-teaching Connection Activity

Activity: Dear "Me" Part 1 and Part 2

Purpose: To become grounded in our personal views, feelings, and vision for ourselves as an individual co-teacher.

Process: Dear "Me" Part 1: Write a letter to yourself about your journey in beccoming an educator. What made you decide to be a teacher? What skills do you have that make you proud to teach and be with students every day? What makes you an effective educator? How do you know?

Dear "Me" Part 2: Transport yourself to the end of the school year. Write to yourself as you are right now. Tell yourself how you hope to experience co-teaching and learning this year. What are you looking forward to? What is important? What actions can you take now and in the coming weeks and months to make your co-teaching vision happen?

Time to Share! Make time to exhange letters with your co-teacher—and then discuss the contents of your letters and your co-teacher's letters. What are some similarities and differences? How each one of you support one another in making your visions be experiences as one powerful co-teaching team?

Book Discussion Questions

1. What is one idea that resonates with you about the CPZ so far?
2. How do you personally connect with the premise of the CPZ?
3. In your opinion what is at least one way that the CPZ can be a possible beacon of hope for experiencing effective and sustainable co-teaching practices?

2
Entering the Motivation Zone

Math was 7th period. Not only was it late in the day when attention to school begins to fade with the anticipation of the end of the school day drawing near, but it was also directly following lunch. Not the ideal schedule. Regardless, the co-teachers knew they needed to model the excitement of learning, with the hopes that their explicit animation would be contagious—at least to some extent. As Mr. Fischer finished reviewing a key math concept, Ms. Brooke power walked over to Mr. Fischer at the front of the class. They shared a smile and a quick high five—and Ms. Brooke took the lead in teaching the next part of the lesson. Mr. Fischer went to the back of the room—clipboard in hand—eyes scanning across the rows. He could see clearly who was purposefully attending and who needed some inconspicuous proximity control to redirect their attention back to the lesson. After this 15-minute segment, Mr. Fischer was up again—with a high five and quick shift between them, Mr. Fischer directed the students to form small groups and Ms. Brooke began to pass out the math materials. As the students worked in groups, both co-teachers walked around the room—making sure that between them—they reached every group. They checked in with one another from across the room to ensure that each group was seen. Ms. Brooke directed the class to come back together, and the teachers took turns sharing specific student examples to review the key concepts of the lesson. Students were invited to add further questions or ideas. During the final moments of class, students submitted their classwork. The period ended as each student wrote one thing that went well and one question they still had on a sticky note. They left their note on their desk and scrambled out of the room as the bell rang. The co-teachers quickly read through the sticky notes, and they noticed most students wrote how "fun" the lesson was—with many students acknowledging the "high fives" as something that went well. Some may critique this as not having anything to do with the content being taught. Yet, the submitted classwork revealed that every student applied the math lesson with evident progress toward individual learning. Based on students' participation, completed work, and feedback from the sticky notes, our high fives, our co-teaching relationship, served as a foundation for creating a culture of belonging, engagement, and inclusivity that permeated through our instructional practices and learning environment. As the bell rang, and students shuffled out of the room to their next class, and so did Ms. Brookes. Only the next co-taught setting was not as lively. The next class was science. Ms. Brookes had so many ideas for actively teaching alongside her co-teacher. Yet, her heart sank over and over again as missed opportunities to be meaningfully active flashed before her eyes. Despite an eagerness to share knowledge, she struggled to contribute. Frankly, she struggled to be seen. Just as in the scenario at the beginning of Chapter 1, the co-teaching relationship with this teacher, in this class, served as a foundation for creating the culture in the classroom—and this culture permeated through the instructional practices and learning environment. In this class, the same four students raised their hands to contribute. Furthermore, the same six students slouched and held their heads up with their hands as their arm fell onto their desktop. The remaining students sat quietly—all following learning behavior protocol: eye contact, upright in their seats, and writing in their notebooks when directed. And there was Ms. Brookes, walking around the room monitoring students' learning. In her mind she rationalized that she was connecting with each student as she walked around. Yet, she felt invisible. There was just no breathable space for her to contribute. The general educator led the class solo. The interesting part was that some of the students were with Ms. Brookes in math class. They went from being active participants to passive learners in the blink of one period. What a difference the co-teaching relationship makes.

The co-teaching power zone considers the reality that co-teachers are individuals with varying degrees of willingness and comfort to co-teach. To make co-teaching work—I mean authentically work—we must honor the motivation behind each co-teacher's reason for co-teaching in the first place. We must value where they are in their feelings about co-teaching, and then guide them toward greater awareness and collaboration. Motivation to co-teach is certainly not something to force—but rather support, scaffold, and expect co-teaching to be a personalized experience that results in both co-teachers making the most of co-creating an effective experience. Since the co-teaching power zone holds relationships at the center of all actions, it is important to increase awareness of each co-teacher's perspective and individual relationship with the idea of co-teaching.

Individual Motivation

The spark of any co-teaching partnership must begin with an understanding of why each individual is co-teaching in the first place. What is the motivation behind their actions? What is their sense of purpose for engaging in co-teaching? Grounded in the roots of self-determination theory (Ryan & Deci, 2017), the co-teaching power zone depends on the intentions and motivations that co-teachers bring to the relationship. Let's consider the role of motivation and amotivation in embracing the celebrations and challenges of any co-teaching pair. Co-teachers join together due to a range of reasons and situations. Some are forced into it as the result of agreed-upon rotation cycles—the "it's your turn this year" situation. Others are simply told because there simply is no other choice. Yet, others are brought together because they seek it out—they, in fact, go to their administrator and say, "We want to co-teach together." Since the co-teaching power zone illustrates that the co-teachers' relationship permeates through the overall culture of the classroom, it is paramount that time cultivating the co-teaching relationship is clear and consistent. In order to co-create the most effective relationship possible, it is vital that each co-teacher identifies what motivates them to act the way they do within their co-teaching experience. To do this, we must first look at each individual and the reasons why they are co-teaching (see Figure 2.1). For co-teaching relationships to grow, let's look at three possible reasons educators co-teach. The amotivated co-teacher is in the partnership because they are told that they must do so. They may not see the value in co-teaching and may prefer teaching solo. They may feel uncomfortable sharing the physical space, their time, and the instructional responsibilities with another teacher. The amotivated co-teacher may simply go through the motions and limit any form of collaboration. The extrinsically motivated co-teacher may be externally regulated, for example, they may be told they must co-teach; yet they engage in co-teaching while being motivated by pleasing administrators, parents, colleagues, and quite simply connecting it to receiving good evaluations. They do what they have to do to fulfill their co-teaching responsibilities. The intrinsically motivated co-teacher is most aware of the value of co-teaching for their own personal and professional growth and their students' performance and achievements. Once established, co-teachers acknowledge where they fall within stage one of the motivation

Amotivated		
May feel forced to co-teach resulting in indifference, reluctance, or avoidance when it comes to working with a co-teacher.	**Extrinsically Motivated**	
	May feel pressured to co-teach; however, will do what they have to do. May exhibit a status quo attitude toward co-teaching.	**Intrinsically Motivated**
		May feel a high degree of personal interest in co-teaching. May show a willingness to work in collaboration with a co-teacher because they see the value in co-teaching.

FIGURE 2.1 Individual Motivation: The Decision to Co-teach.

zone. At this moment in time, where do you fall along the individual motivation process? This is your baseline. Once identified, rest in that awareness and be proud of what you stand for as an educator—whatever that may be. Now that you connect with your baseline motivation, you decide what you want your max line to be. How may you evolve with your current motivation status and move toward your maximum performance as a co-teacher?

As we value the reason why each co-teacher is in their specific partnership, we can understand the reasons for their particular actions toward co-teaching. This is the entry point for valuing each teacher's perspective, finding solutions, and entering the second stage of the motivation zone.

How Motivated Are You?

After identifying one's individual motivation stance, they are ready to embrace the partnership. The emphasis on "co" first happens here. The motivation zone illustrates a continuous sequence of possible attitudes toward co-teaching that takes the amotivated, externally motivated, or intrinsically motivated co-teaching pair to the next steps in finding personalized solutions to make their co-teaching experience more efficient. Figure 2.2 illustrates the range of possibilities that describe any co-teaching pairing as we move from individual perceptions and motivations (see Figure 2.1) to the partnership. We see how the

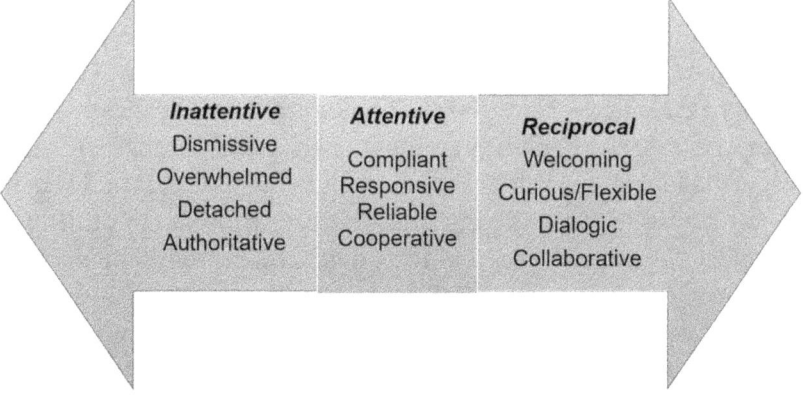

FIGURE 2.2 Co-teaching Motivation Zone: Partnership Reality.

amotivated, external, and intrinsic motivations often transfer into actions ranging from inattentive, attentive, and reciprocal co-teaching experiences. The adjacent descriptors reveal a flow from quite uncooperative and avoidant to mutually collaborative and engaging. You will also notice the outer extremes of the continuum describe co-teaching experiences that are quite distinct.

Motivation sets the foundation to bring awareness and value to the perspectives and experiences of each co-teacher. It moves one's motivation to co-teach (see Figure 2.1) and brings it to the next level of co-teaching actions.

Inattentive: The inattentive experience describes at least one co-teacher who avoids engaging in the collaborative process needed for effective co-teaching. It may be the general educator who may have a difficult time sharing the physical classroom space and the instructional time. Furthermore, one co-teacher may apply binary language that results in feelings of exclusion rather than inclusion. For example, a teacher may use language such as "my class," "my students," "your students," etc. One teacher, typically the special educator, feels like a visitor in the classroom, often feeling invisible as the general education co-teacher dismisses the notion of sharing the teaching and learning process. One or both teachers may feel overwhelmed by the degree of responsibility it takes to collaborate.

Attentive: The attentive experience illustrates a pairing that works well or well enough. They meet the requirements of co-teaching, however, and do not go beyond what the job entails. For example, they cooperate with one another, but sometimes one or both teachers feel the pressure of their responsibilities. The general educator may feel the pull of additional time to plan or may feel that working with another teacher takes time away from teaching the content in a manner they feel is most efficient. Nevertheless, they cooperate and "allow" the special educator to contribute to the teaching and learning process. In addition, the special educator may feel fortunate to work with a cooperative co-teacher yet is met with frustration at times because they feel as though they must fit into the general education process. Therefore, they may feel as though their teaching style is not fully experienced as they give way to the way to their co-teacher's way of teaching. Regardless, attentive co-teaching experiences honor both co-teachers as they compromise and communicate to stay in compliance with policies and procedures that comprise a co-taught classroom.

Reciprocal: The reciprocal co-teaching experience exemplifies the mutuality of honoring each co-teacher's perspective, experiences, and expertise. Each co-teacher values the act of co-teaching itself while acknowledging the value of one another. They move beyond simply agreeing in cooperation to a more enriching way of learning from and with one another with curiosity to share and learn new ways of teaching and learning. Communication is transparent and ongoing. There is a mutual desire to teach and learn alongside one another and their students. Cooperation moves to true collaboration which further values one another and their contributions to the classroom. They speak and act in terms of "our students" and are open and willing to be flexible in the ways they design instruction. They are open to learning with one another as they meet the strengths and needs of all learners. Acknowledging each co-teacher's stance is key moving toward collaboration. Take the time you need to find where you are along this continuum. As you confidently and courageously acknowledge where you are—you will first accept that place, and then be ready to take responsibility for your actions and willingness to learn in collaboration as you are ready. See Part 2, Chapter 4 for collaborating in the co-teaching power zone and its unique process of illuminating the need to connect, disconnect, and reconnect to allow co-teachers to be in the zone. For now, let's continue with the critical awareness for co-teachers to individually connect with their willingness to engage in their role as a co-teacher.

According to Ryan and Deci (2017), there are three basic needs within the self-determination theory that are the "nutrients that are essential for growth, integrity, and well-being" (p. 10). According to over 40 years of research, an individual's willingness to act and engage within the environment comes down to these three basic needs and is true across all human beings, cultures, and anywhere humans gather (Deci & Ryan, 2000). The three basic needs that have shown predictive value in supporting effective human actions include every individual's need for autonomy, competence, and relatedness in a given social environment (Ryan & Deci, 2017). Are you feeling the co-teaching value here? Yes, co-teachers need to be autonomous, feel competent as they actively contribute, and they need to relate to one another, their students, and the overall process of co-teaching. In fact, these three basic human needs serve as a guiding light as we support co-teachers to live within their personal co-teaching power zone.

Three Basic Needs for Effective Co-teaching

The co-teaching power zone framework upholds a commitment to working with others by first and foremost connecting with our own perspective. The idea is that as we increase our awareness of our view of ourselves as a co-teacher, we can then communicate and collaborate with others more effectively. The co-teaching power zone is structured to optimize learning and growing alongside one another as co-teachers. First, each individual teacher must identify the extent to which they feel autonomous, competent, and related within the context of their co-teaching situation. These concepts were briefly defined in the introduction, and now it's time for us to take a deeper look into how they apply to the classroom.

Autonomy: The co-teacher is willing to co-teach and personally endorses their own actions. They experience a high degree of interest in co-teaching. Co-teachers who are intrinsically motivated, clearly, feel autonomous. However, if a co-teacher is externally motivated, but willing to go along with the co-teaching assignment, they may still feel autonomous. If the co-teacher feels forced and amotivated by external pressure, a sense of autonomy may likely be tenuous. The question becomes: *How may we support co-teachers to feel autonomous from the onset of assigning them to their co-teaching role?* Let's move into the classroom. For the basic need of autonomy to be met, both teachers need to feel active and willing to participate in the instructional process.

Competence: Co-teachers feel capable and effectively engaged. Their actions are based on a belief that they have the skillset needed within the social context of the classroom. Consistent with the self-determination theory, the motivation zone guides co-teachers to embrace their competencies in a process, growth-oriented manner. Competence is a process that goes beyond achieving an outcome. Competence is embraced with a willingness to continue learning and improving one's skills.

Relatedness: For co-teachers to work optimally together, each feels a sense of belonging with a feeling of "I matter and make a difference." Each teacher feels valued with opportunities to meaningfully contribute within the learning environment and instructional process.

When each co-teacher embraces their motivational stance for co-teaching, they take the first step in entering their personalized co-teaching power zone. Communication can begin to acknowledge and support each co-teacher as they share their experience in feeling motivated, autonomous, competent, and related to all aspects of the co-teaching partnership. The focus on how each co-teacher currently experiences each need serves as an entry point for improving (hence, transforming) each co-teaching experience. The next chapter begins to branch out from the focus on developing your roots, your self-awareness, self-motivation, and ideas about co-teaching toward considering yourself in partnership with your co-teacher.

Co-teaching Check-in: Three Basic Co-teaching Needs

This activity is meant to be an ongoing process. To support transparent, consistent communication this basic needs check-in could do wonders in creating personalized, effective co-teaching experiences. To ensure this happens for you, consider the need for consistency in engaging in this check-in activity every 6–8 weeks (or sooner!) to ensure you and your co-teacher are making the absolute most of your opportunity to co-teach together. I recommend the first completion session should be after the first 2–4 weeks of school to get that baseline—while also having some time together. When this activity is repeated throughout the year, it will be exciting to see how you two evolve together to transform your co-teaching world. Once you and your co-teacher respond individually, remember to discuss your responses together and consider any changes that need to be made to continue to support one another.

1. **Autonomous:** On a scale of one to five, where five is the greatest, 1. How autonomous do you feel as a co-teacher? 2. Do you feel in charge of your own co-teaching actions or are there times when you are simply going through the motions? Be specific by providing an example.
2. **Competent:** On a scale of one to five, where five is the greatest, 1. How competent do you feel as a co-teacher? Do you feel you are contributing to all phases of the co-teaching process in meaningful ways? 2. What is one way you would like to add to your contributions as a co-teacher? 3. How may your co-teacher support you in contributing in ongoing, meaningful ways? Share an example to express how you feel.
3. **Relatedness:** On a scale of one to five, where five is the greatest, 1. How valued do you feel by and with your co-teaching partner? 2. Do you feel that your presence and co-teaching actions make a difference within the classroom learning environment? Be specific by providing an example of an exchange between you and your

co-teacher—or a classroom example. What is one way your co-teacher may support you feeling valued as an active member of the teaching and learning process in your classroom?

As you connect with the three basic needs, you are automatically tapping into your personal power. In fact, you are illuminating your co-teaching truths as a necessary step toward branching out in partnership with your co-teacher.

Personal Co-teaching Truth

Remember, you and your co-teacher must belong to one another first and foremost for the most effective co-teaching practices to unfold into the instructional process and overall learning environment. However, for you and your co-teacher to belong with one another, you must continue to check-in with your view of yourself as a co-teacher. This is the time to revisit all activities within this section of the book. Honor wherever you are within the motivation zone. Remember do not force yourself to be in a place where you are not—just let the process flow as you stay committed to be within the comfort of your personalized co-teaching power zone. The following tools will empower you as you settle into the CPZ:

1. Speaking your co-teaching truth: This activity encourages you to stay true to yourself.
2. The conscious co-teaching action planner: This activity encourages you to begin to blend your truths in partnership within your co-teaching experience.

Key Takeaways

- The co-teaching partnership begins by each co-teacher considering their motivation to co-teach.
- Three possible co-teaching motivations exist and lay the groundwork for cultivating an effective and sustainable relationship.
- The motivation zone invites co-teachers to explore their personal and collective motivation for co-teaching.
- The aim of a motivated partnership is for co-teachers to practice reciprocity along the process of their actions, interactions, and communication processes.
- When teaching within the co-teaching power zone, co-teachers experience a sense of having three basic human needs met. Each co-teacher feels autonomous, competent, and related within instructional process and learning environment.

Co-teaching Connection Activity #2: Your Co-teaching Truths

This brief, but empowering activity provides the opportunity for you to connect with and express your inner voice of truth. It can be a powerful source of confidence that validates your beliefs and experiences as you work to cultivate and sustain a relationship with your co-teacher. The idea is that an effective relationship with your co-teacher begins with your connection with yourself—your true self. When you engage in your co-teaching truths, you minimize or eliminate the possibility of external influences to sway your personal sense of worthiness. Speaking your co-teaching truth supports personal empowerment and branches out toward honest, transparent, and reciprocal co-teaching relationships. The idea is if you hold back your co-teaching truth, you will likely experience more frustration, resentment, disconnection, dissatisfaction, and internal conflict. Connecting with your co-teaching truths expands opportunities to create healthy boundaries and dynamic co-teaching relationships. To connect simply respond to the following activity.

Activity: Getting Grounded with Our Shared Vision (Stein, 2016, 2023)

This activity provides an opportunity to create the roots for a strong co-teaching year together. First, each co-teacher considers their response to each question and then spends quality time sharing their beliefs with one another at a convenient time soon following individual reflections.

Each co-teacher should document their individual response and the response of their co-teacher.

After answering and discussing all questions, the co-teachers should highlight the themes that arise in all responses. From these themes, from combining all responses, co-teachers should create a shared vision statement(s). This shared vision will be agreed upon by both teachers and displayed in a place where they are reminded of this connection throughout the year.

Thoughtful question	*Your response*	*Your co-teacher's response*
1. What is the teacher's role in supporting individual student's learning?		
2. What is the optimal classroom learning environment?		
3. What are your personal strengths as an educator? How do your talents/expertise optimize students' learning?		
4. What do you think is the best way to support students' learning differences?		

Shared Vision Statement: _____

_____

Book Study Questions

1. What role do you feel motivation plays in creating an effective co-teaching partnership?
2. Share one idea or example of how motivation impacts the effectiveness of a co-teaching partnership?
3. How do you think the degree of individual and collective motivation between co-teachers impacts instruction and the overall classroom learning environment? Be specific.

3

Using the Conscious Co-teacher Action Planner

This is the point within the CPZ process, that you will begin to extend your understanding of how your personal perspective and experiences blend with your co-teaching partner's view of co-teaching. This chapter guides a necessary and deeper sense of self (and being) that is needed to allow for that natural flow in strengthening and creating the roots to experience a sense of belonging with your co-teacher. Remember, to enter and create a meaningful co-teaching power zone experience, you must have the roots for a strong, evolving sense of self. This interactive chapter invites you to first step into your own power as you remember to stay connected with your own co-teaching truth. The chapter then invites you and your co-teaching partner to complete the Conscious Co-teacher Action Planner individually. Then set up a time using the cogenerative dialogue format (see Chapter 7) to collegially discuss and share your individual perspectives. The idea to consider here is what actions may you each take to improve your co-teaching experience? How may each of you support one another in ways that make you each feel autonomous, competent, and valued in relation to and with one another? First, let's connect with your authentic co-teaching self.

DOI: 10.4324/9781003333692-5

The Conscious Co-teaching Action Planner

Current perspective and practices	Actions I will take
Refer to Figure 2.1: Individual Motivation. What are your reasons for co-teaching? What are the extrinsic reasons that spark your current co-teaching role? What are your current intrinsic reasons? Where are you along the individual motivation continuum?	What is one thing you may do to increase your motivation to co-teach with your current co-teaching partner?
Refer to Figure 2.2: The Partnership Reality Where do you personally find yourself? Are you inattentive, attentive, or ready for reciprocity? What are the reasons you find yourself in this particular place along the continuum at this time?	Looking ahead, where could and should you and your co-teacher broaden your thinking around teaching with reciprocity?
What is one example of a choice you make to interact with vision, intention, and communication with your co-teacher?	Review the description of being attentive and teaching with reciprocity. Select one or two ways you may personally act to interact with our co-teacher?

Key Takeaways

- ♦ To optimize a co-teaching partnership, the motivation zone invites each co-teacher to connect with their current sense of self and their willingness to personally grow and evolve within their co-teaching experience.
- ♦ The motivation zone within the CPZ provides the opportunity for co-teachers to become more aware of their personal perspectives and seek to understand their co-teacher's point of view.
- ♦ The conscious co-teaching action planning tool allows each co-teacher to consider their actions and the possible ways they may contribute toward improving their co-teaching experience for and with their co-teaching partner.

Co-teaching Connection Activity #3: Transformative Plan

Purpose: To increase self-awareness and begin to learn from and with one another. This activity provides the opportunity to improve co-teaching relationships and the overall instructional process and learning environment.

Process: Sketch out the graphic below (Figure 3.1) and respond to each question. Once complete, remember to share your responses with your co-teacher, and see how you can transform your personal and collective co-teaching moves!

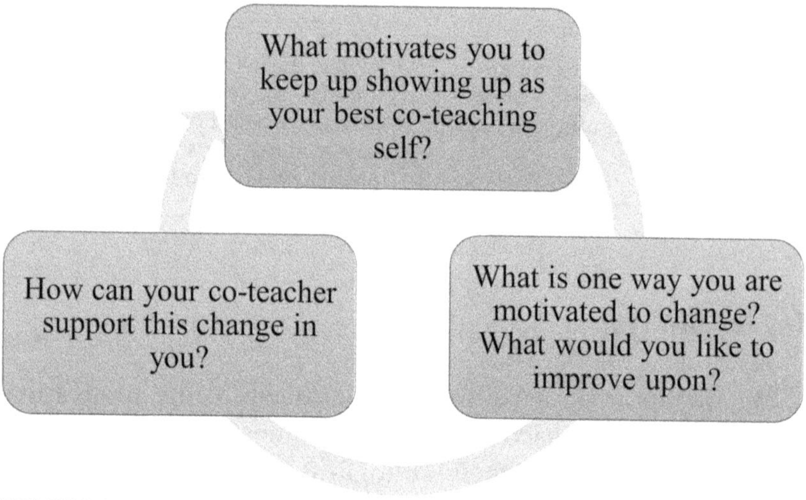

- What motivates you to keep up showing up as your best co-teaching self?
- How can your co-teacher support this change in you?
- What is one way you are motivated to change? What would you like to improve upon?

FIGURE 3.1 Transforming Co-teaching Experiences

Book Discussion Questions

- Why do you think it is important for each co-teacher to reflect on their personal co-teaching truth?
- How can a stronger sense of self help a co-teacher connect more efficiently with their co-teacher?
- Review the consious co-teaching action planner tool, and explain two ways it can optimize the process of building a strong co-teaching foundation.

We Just Click! Co-teaching Character Action: Inspire
Earn Your Motivation Jigsaw Puzzle Piece

After completing the chapter reading, book club questions, and activities so far, you are ready to earn a co-teaching connection puzzle piece!

Consider your personal motivation for co-teaching in your current assignment. Look back at Figures 2.1 and Figure 2.2 in Chapter 2 to support your thinking.

Where do you find yourself along the continuum of the motivation zone? Acknowledge how you feel about co-teaching by accepting where you are along the continuum. How do you experience the three basic needs? Do not place judgment on where you land along the continuum—embrace it! Celebrate it! This is an acknowledgment to value how you are coming into this co-teaching partnership from the start. Are you willing to evolve and commit to the best possible partnership reality with your current co-teacher?

This authentic awareness is your entry point for engaging in the best possible partnership with your current co-teacher. Embrace the understanding that each co-teaching pairing will likely feel different from previous experiences. At this point, just focus on YOU. Be blatantly honest with yourself as you complete the Conscious Co-teacher Action Planner. What inspires you to accept and experience your current co-teaching role? Share your honest reflections with your co-teacher and begin to inspire one another!

We Just Click! Congratulations! It is time to celebrate! You earned your Inspire Jigsaw puzzle piece! After the two of you share your action planner responses and understand your own perspective and the perspective of the other, make a copy of the Inspire puzzle piece in the appendix and display in a prominent place that is a visual reminder of co-teaching pride for each of you each day.

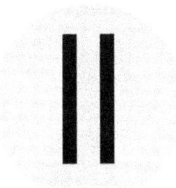

Belonging
The Collaboration Zone

Chapter 4: Ramping Up Collaboration by Connecting, Disconnecting, and Reconnecting

Chapter 5: Increasing Collaboration with the Co-teaching Models

4
Ramping Up Collaboration by Connecting, Disconnecting, and Reconnecting

The Co-teaching Power Zone (CPZ) Framework illuminates the naturally wide range of collaborative opportunities that co-teachers may experience. You know what I mean. We have personally experienced or heard stories about teachers who finish each other's sentences and flexibly make the most of whatever co-planning time they have together. Across the full range of collaborative options, we also know how many co-teachers experience that loud, uncomfortable silence of disharmony. We know that just putting two teachers in the room does not instantly guarantee co-teaching will occur in the best possible way. Enter the CPZ Framework.

The CPZ Framework honors every experience. It does not force any two co-teachers together—it embraces human existence and varying perspectives—and then works to improve the co-teaching process from that point of reality. That point of reality—whatever that may be—is the personalized co-teaching launching pad on a natural path toward improvement. Co-teachers have the natural conditions for making true collaboration happen—simply because they are consistently in the same room together—so why not make the most of it. That brings us to the question: What is *true* collaboration?

DOI: 10.4324/9781003333692-7

Collaborating in the Co-teaching Power Zone

Research has long defined collaboration as the key to effective co-teaching (Friend & Bursuck, 2002, 2012; Honigsfeld & Dove, 2008; Dove & Honigsfeld, 2017; Murawski & Spencer, 2011).

According to Friend and Cook (2003) collaboration is based on mutual goals and shared responsibility for decision making and participation within all phases of the instructional process. Co-teaching calls for active involvement from both teachers; however, in practice, co-teachers often struggle to experience the intention of collaboration (Scruggs et al., 2007; Pugach & Winn, 2011). Co-teaching also optimizes opportunities to embrace the naturally embedded growth that co-teachers may experience both personally and professionally as teachers learn from and with one another (McDuffie et al., 2009; Sandholtz, 2000).

Within the CPZ Framework, the collaboration zone brings awareness to a natural process of collaboration that brings unique addition to our understanding of collaboration.

Specifically, there is a natural flow of connecting, disconnecting, and reconnecting experienced between every co-teaching pair. The collaboration zone honors a unique process of reciprocal collaboration that honors and supports the unique abilities

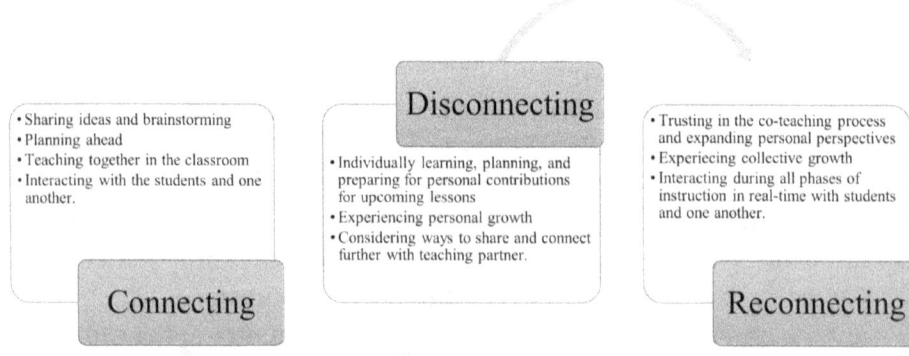

FIGURE 4.1 Connecting, Disconnecting, and Reconnecting.

of each co-teacher. Figure 4.1 illustrates the natural process of mutual collaboration within the CPZ Framework.

Co-teachers begin by connecting as they share their ideas and begin to get an idea for how their unique beliefs and skills will blend with their teaching partner's skills and views on co-teaching. Connecting must illuminate the time each co-teacher needs to express their contributions as a co-teacher. The collaboration zone shines a light on the natural and necessary process of disconnecting, so each co-teacher may work on personal tasks that either helps them to prepare personally or professionally for their lessons and time in class together. Disconnected tasks may include time where the co-teacher connects with other colleagues, learns on their own by researching or participating in professional learning activities, plans their part of a lesson, or reads through students' files or individualized education plan (IEP) in connection with upcoming lessons. The collaboration zone within the CPZ Framework explains the value of focusing on ways the co-teachers must come together, move apart, and then come back together in new and transformed ways as they share their knowledge and perspectives. The reconnecting is the pivotal moment. This is the time when co-teachers come back together to share what they learned and thought about since they last connected. This part takes trust, patience, and an open mind for each co-teacher to learn from and with one another. In time, these are the very moments that guide transformative co-teaching practices. In the spirit of embracing co-teaching realities, there is a range of possible ways for co-teachers to experience this collaboration flow. Each range acts as a launching pad for co-teachers to improve their personalized practices—together.

Table 4.1 shares four possible stages co-teachers may experience along the collaboration zone within the CPZ. Notice the flow of possibilities here. The range of stages moves between the realities of two teachers who share a physical space by being in the same room, but they do not interact in meaningful ways on a consistent basis. The next stage describes a cooperative relationship where, although inconsistent, two teachers work together "well enough." The students are often quiet and hesitant to participate. The next stage flows into the kind of collaboration

TABLE 4.1 Four possible phases of the collaboration continuum

Phase one: singular	Co-teaching practices exhibit little or limited evidence of planful and intentional teacher interactions. A typical lesson on any given day shares one teacher teaching the class as the teaching partner stands off to the side and silently walks around the room supporting students as needed.
Phase two: cooperative	Professional practices reflect evidence of shared responsibility to meet the requirements of co-teaching. One co-teacher may be more cooperative, but both co-teachers express some degree of acknowledgment in working together to meet the needs of the students in their classroom. These two teachers are able to "get the job done" when there is a visitor in the room. However, consistent collaboration is not always within reach.
Phase three: collaborative:	Both co-teachers display a willingness to co-teach. There is evidence of a mutual trust and commitment to supporting one another as they focus on guiding all students to achieve in their classroom. The students feel a friendly, collegial tone in the classroom.
Phase four: reciprocal	Professional practices illuminate a mutual trust and comprehensive process interaction that includes the necessity to connect, disconnect, and reconnect to strengthen their collaborations and sense of belonging as their position as a co-teacher is mutually valued. Both teachers are interested and willing to continuously improve their co-teaching practices.

co-teachers, researchers, and all stakeholders dream about. The students engage in cooperative learning and interact with their peers with the aim of completing a task. In the collaborative stage, mutual trust finally enters the scene. This is the classroom where the students feel the flow of connected energy between their two teachers. The relationship between the two teachers is contagious in that the students are engaged and feel comfortable to actively participate, ask questions, and be a part of a lively classroom community. In fact, all visitors feel a sense of meaningful collaboration and autonomous co-teaching. Just when you think it couldn't get any better, the CPZ Framework introduces the possibility of the reciprocal stage. This stage includes all aspects of the collaborative stage but introduces the notion and need for the co-teachers to acknowledge the ways they connect, disconnect, and reconnect to further empower themselves and one another. In fact, the students also feel and enjoy this flexible, yet structured flow of learning. For example, they engage in dialogue easily with peers, work independently when needed, and actively participate in individual, small group and whole class learning.

The four stages along the collaboration zone become enmeshed within a natural process of co-teaching that illuminates the ways co-teachers experience a sense of being, belonging, and power because their relationship permeates through their instruction and learning environment.

Table 4.2 illustrates a range of possibilities for how co-teachers may apply their sense of self and motivation to co-teach along the possible stages of co-teaching. The collaboration zone provides the information and language needed to guide the teaching partners to come together to acknowledge where they live within the continuum of the collaboration zone. It provides the language to guide their transparent communications as they have the opportunity to strive to keep improving through dialogue and shared actions. Once they establish their current co-teaching stage, they move along to see how their relationship impacts their instructional process (see Table 4.3) and then identify how their current relationship impacts their learning environment (see Table 4.4).

This collaboration zone allows for dynamic interactions between the co-teachers that results in opportunities for building and sustaining meaningful relationships. The co-teachers' relationship, in turn, permeates through to impact their instructional practices and the co-creation of their learning environment. The impact their relationship has on instruction and the learning environment is intentional as co-teachers become more aware of the complexities of co-teaching by considering where their relationship stands, and how their relationship impacts instruction and the learning environment. The collaboration zone, and the overall CPZ framework, offers a guide for co-teachers to identify specific areas of strength and specific areas that could be

TABLE 4.2 Being along the collaboration zone

Singular	Cooperative	Collaborative	Reciprocal
• One or both teachers feel hesitant, guarded, or unwilling to co-teach. • They "get through" each day with limited communication.	• At least one co-teacher commits to co-teaching. • Evidence supports they meet co-teaching requirements. • Intermittent communication.	• Both co-teachers are willing to co-teach. • They support one another. • Mutual trust and shared responsibility. • Transparent communication.	• Mutual trust and sense of belonging within their teaching partnership. • Transparent communication. • Comprehensive collaborative relationship to include connecting, disconnecting, and reconnecting.

TABLE 4.3 Belonging within instructional process

Singular	Cooperative	Collaborative	Reciprocal
• One co-teacher dominates as lead teacher. • Limited to no evidence of applying or varying the co-teaching models. • Students sit quietly at their seats. • It is a challenge to meet the needs of the varying student abilities during instructional time. • Co-teachers do not usually agree on instructional strategies. • Co-teachers may divide responsibility of students rather than working together for and with all students.	• Both co-teachers involved in the teaching, yet one may dominate more often. • One or both co-teachers may sometimes feel they could do more to support instruction for students. • Some evidence of co-teaching models. • Most of the students participate in teacher-directed tasks. • At least one teacher works toward supporting unique student abilities and needs. • Beginning to discuss their shared responsibility for teaching all students.	• Both teachers consistently contribute in meaningful and unique ways. • Each co-teacher feels valued and confident in their abilities and actions. • Students feel comfortable to actively participate in peer discussions in small group and whole class discussions. • Student-directed learning is balanced with teacher-directed lessons. • Both teachers share the responsibility to implement instructional strategies to support the varying abilities and needs in their class.	• Both co-teachers are active participants. • Each teacher leads aspects of lesson(s). • Evidence of varying co-teaching models. • Co-teachers value each other's contributions. • Co-teachers have increased self-awareness and work together to continually improve their practices. • Co-teachers mindfully engage in a process of connecting, disconnecting, and reconnecting as they each contribute specific strategies and procedures to empower all learners.

TABLE 4.4 Power learning environment

Singular	Cooperative	Collaborative	Reciprocal
• One co-teacher enforces the class rules. • One co-teacher may feel uncomfortable and stifled. • Students may feel one teacher is in charge and the teaching partner is there to help. • Students are compliant or engage with one teacher more than the other.	• Both co-teachers enforce the class rules; however, one may enforce simply to honor their co-teacher. • One co-teacher may feel they have to ask permission from their co-teacher rather than share their ideas about class procedures. • Students comply with possible more engagement as two teachers begin to work together.	• Both teachers create and enforce the class rules/procedures together. • Teaching partners naturally model open communication, ask each other for their thoughts, and make decisions together throughout the day. • Students feel they have two teachers who they may go to equally for questions regarding classroom procedures and rules. • Students are more actively engaged in peer collaborations.	• Both teachers enjoy a mutual trust and sense of belonging to and with one another as evidenced by their structured and relaxed way of working together. • Each teacher feels comfortable to add their thoughts and opinions throughout the day. • A strong, harmonious balance of teacher-led and student-led activities are present • Each teacher is consistently active in their personal role and together as a teaching partnership.

improved upon. The result is a process of transformation that will keep co-teachers evolving with their relationship with one another and the impact they have on their instructional practices and creating their classroom culture within the learning environment. This collaboration zone may be a topic of discussion for one of their scheduled cogenerative dialogues in Part 3. For now, let's move to co-teaching models as a collaborative tool for designing instruction.

Key Takeaways

- ♦ Research acknowledges collaboration as the key to effective co-teaching relationships
- ♦ The CPZ expands the current view of co-teaching collaboration by introducing the presence of the natural process of connecting, disconnecting, and reconnecting for cultivating strong, growth-fostering co-teaching relationships.
- ♦ The collaboration zone, within the CPZ, offers four phases that reveal a continuum of possible co-teaching experiences. The ultimate goal is to experience reciprocal and mutual ways of being, trusting, and caring together along the teaching and learning process.
- ♦ The collaboration continuum supports co-teachers to increase their awareness of how they are experiencing collaboration with one another. The continuum is a tool that keeps co-teachers in the collaboration zone as they move through being, belonging, and power experiences within the CPZ.
- ♦ The collaboration zone provides opportunities for dynamic interactions between co-teachers.
- ♦ The collaboration zone (and the CPZ as a whole) optimizes opportunities for transformative co-teaching practices to unfold as co-teachers learn from and with one another along a reciprocal and dialogic process.

Co-teaching Connection Activity: Colorful Co-teaching Realities

Colorful Co-teaching Realities

Break out the crayons or colored pencils! Then read the titles below each shape and choose a color to express how you feel about each. As you color each shape, consider why you chose that specific color. How do you feel about that particular aspect of your co-teaching experience? How does your selected color make you feel? How does your selected color align, or not align, with your feelings? Feel free to jot words down to add words or symbols next to, or inside, each shape to briefly explain how you are feeling about each title listed. Be ready to share with your co-teacher!

Your role as a co-teacher

Your co-teacher's role

Your current co-planning process

Meeting students' strengths and needs

The instructional process and class management

Being a part of creating the learning environment

Stein, E., 2023

FIGURE 4.2 Colorful Co-teaching Realities

Book Discussion Questions

1. Draw a sketch to show the ongoing, organic flow of connecting, disconnecting, and reconnecting within a meaningful collaborative loop within the CPZ framework. Share your visual and explain with your co-teaching partner. How are your explanations the same and different?
2. What is the most important aspect you want to remember about this dynamic and transformative process of connecting, disconnecting, and reconnecting? How does it empower stronger collaborations between you and your co-teaching partner?
3. The collaboration zone provides opportunities for dynamic co-teaching actions and interactions. Describe or list three to five examples of specific dynamic actions and interactions that may unfold when you and your co-teacher are well within the collaboration zone.

5

Increasing Collaboration with the Co-teaching Models

The co-teaching models serve as a structure that teachers need to guide meaningful, and varied, collaborations. There are six different ways teachers may organize their teaching together with plenty of flexibility within the structure for teachers to apply their personal teaching styles and strategies According to Friend and Cook (1992), co-teaching in special education is a service delivery model where a general educator shares the responsibility of planning, instructional delivery, and assessment with a special educator for a group of students that include students with disabilities. "In co-teaching, the teachers strive to create a classroom community in which all students are valued members, and they develop innovative strategies that would not be possible if only one teacher was present" (p. 1). Evolving definitions continue to stay focused on what is most important when implementing co-teaching. "Co-teaching occurs when two or more professionals jointly deliver substantive instruction to a diverse, blended group of students, primarily in a single physical space" (Friend & Cook, 2017, p. 163). Let's spend some time accentuating four critical components (Cook & Friend, 1995, p. 2):

   a) **Two educators** include one general educator and one special educator or other special services provider such as speech/language therapist. The focus is on including the unique possibilities that may unfold when two different, but complementary perspectives come together to provide instruction to a group of students with varying abilities. The role of each teacher includes: The general educator specializes in the curriculum, pacing, and structuring lessons. The special educator (or related service provider) contributes strategies that align with unique learning needs and abilities of specific students.

Friend and Cook identified related service providers who may co-teach with the general educators including ELL teachers, speech/language therapists, and other general and specialized educators. Although this book's focus is on a general and special educator pairing, the CPZ may easily be applied to support any two teachers teaching and learning together in the same classroom.

b) **Delivering substantive instruction** emphasizes that both teachers should be active, meaningful contributors in all aspects of the instructional process.

c) **Diverse groups of students** refer to students with disabilities. In addition, this book includes the understanding that diverse learners refer to the varying abilities of the individual students within groups of learners in any classroom (Meyer et al., 2014; Stein, 2016, 2023). The special educator ensures that the needs of students with individual education plans (IEPs) are met within the general education classroom in collaboration with the general educator.

d) **Single classroom or physical space** explains the ongoing intention of the two teachers to work together with all students in the same instructional space to ensure an inclusive learning environment where students and teachers create the opportunity for every learner to feel like a valued member of the classroom community (Stein, 2016, 2021, 2023).

Let's extend our understanding of co-teaching by outlining the possible roles of each teacher along the shared process. Co-teachers' participation needs to be considered within the unique partnerships. There is no checklist or formula that can determine how specific tasks should be shared across all co-teaching pairings (Friend, 2016). However, there are general topics that should be considered:

- **Shared Vision**: Discuss and formulate a shared philosophy of teaching and learning. See the activity in the Appendix: Getting Grounded with our Shared Vision.
- **Sharing Space**: How will the classroom be set up to send a clear message that two teachers are in this room! Consider all possible ways to create a sense of belonging for both teachers. This could be simply putting both teachers name on the door, teachers' desks, creating bulletin boards that both teachers have creative contributions.
- **Communication**: How will you create a consistent flow of open and transparent communication? What are the opportunities for in person and virtual, synchronous, and asynchronous modes of communication?
- **Active Participation from both teachers** (Stein, 2016, 2023)

Figure 5.1 is a generalized list of possible ways the roles of each teacher may be visible within the unique, organic flow of their co-teaching partnership.

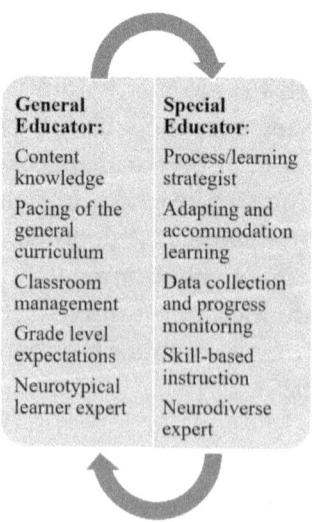

FIGURE 5.1 Possible Co-teaching Roles.

Notice the movement of the arrows demonstrates shared decisions and responsibilities between the two teachers. Depending on the unique pairings, co-teachers may flow back and forth between these roles. Yet, this figure demonstrates a general place to start in ensuring that each teacher contributes in meaningful and necessary ways. In addition, common decisions about the roles of each teacher will need to occur. For example:

1. Who will make decisions about classroom routines and procedures?
2. How will the behavior management process unfold? What part does each teacher play?
3. How will the instructional process be shared? Specifically, what are the options for each teacher to be actively involved in all aspects of the teaching and learning process?
4. How will each teacher be involved in assessment and grading?

These are examples of some common questions that must be discussed, decided, and experienced within consistent ways. The CPZ and general contents of this book will support co-teachers in responding to these and other important questions to build collaborative relationships.

The collaboration zone within the CPZ is an ever-evolving awareness and flow of being, belonging, and power dynamics that weaves through everything the two co-teachers think and do.

As we consider co-teaching roles that include a clear sense of being, belonging, and negotiating power, the six co-teaching models (Friend & Reising, 1993; Friend & Cook, 2007) structure our options for allowing our co-teaching relationship to meaningfully impact instruction and the learning environment.

Within the process of strong co-teaching relationships, a variety of co-teaching models must be applied to maximize the expertise and active participation of both teachers. This shared instructional approach optimizes accessible and meaningful learning for every learner in the room—including the two teachers (Stein, 2016, 2017,

Being: Being refers to a co-teacher's self-view of themselves as learners, educators, and overall human being. The CPZ supports each co-teacher to have a clear, confident sense of their personal strengths and abilities. They become aligned with their motivation to co-teach and their willingness to participate in co-creating the best possible co-teaching partnership possible in each unique situation. They apply these abilities in collaboration with their co-teaching partner.

Belonging: Baumeister and Leary (1995) describe a sense of belonging as the extent in which individuals feel included, accepted, and supported by others within social contexts (Allen et al., 2022). Maslow (2013) explains sense of belonging as an innate psychological drive to belong within groups. Furthermore, Goodenow and Grady (1993) found that when learners experienced a sense of belonging in their classroom, they felt more motivated to participate, had higher expectations for their personal success, and valued their contributions in the classroom environment. The benefits of belonging in the classroom may clearly lead to increased engagement and personal well-being. Yet, *how* teachers may foster a sense of belonging is less understood (Slaten et al., 2016; Stein, 2021, p. 31). The CPZ is, to the best of my knowledge, the first and only co-teaching framework that illuminates *how* to co-create a culture of belonging with co-teachers and students in any co-taught classroom.

Power: As described earlier in this book, the process of the CPZ defines power as shared experiences that transform co-teaching actions and interactions as two co-teachers increase their awareness of their personal strengths and abilities while co-creating opportunities to learn from and with one another. Each co-teacher has the opportunity to experience a sense of belonging as each is an active, valued participant and contributor within all phases of the instructional process.

2023). The six co-teaching models that still remain the most widely used source today are the models identified back in the early 1990s (Cook & Friend, 1993; Friend & Cook, 2007).

- ♦ **Team Teaching**: Both teachers are delivering the same lesson at the same time in the same space. Each teacher contributes in meaningful ways.
- ♦ **One Teach, One Observe**: One teacher is responsible for teaching the class while the teaching partner quietly observes one or more students to gain valuable data on students' performance.
- ♦ **One Teach, One Circulate**: One teacher has the primary responsibility for teaching while the teaching partner circulates the room to quietly support learners as needed.

- **Station Teaching**: Teaching partners create 3–4 instructional activities that work toward specific learning objectives. Each teacher plans and facilitates one activity while one or two other groups work independently or in student-led learning. The students rotate between the groups within time intervals selected by the teachers.
- **Alternative Teaching**: One teacher leads the whole class lesson, and the teaching partner leads a small group instruction. The small group instruction may provide additional support in alignment with the whole class lesson. Another option is for the small group instruction to be either a pre-teaching or re-teaching of specific skill(s) the students need to fill in their personal gaps in learning. The purpose here is to provide students with the skills needed for them to access learning when they are in future whole class lessons.
- **Parallel Teaching**: The teaching team divides the class into two groups. Each partner teaches one of the groups. Both teachers teach the same content, yet they have the flexibility to personalize the instruction to the particular group of students and honor their individual teaching skills and style.

The first three models empower the flow during whole class lessons. The remaining three models guide small group instruction. Teachers select the co-teaching model in the context of specific lessons. The idea is to vary the models to keep the learning flow meaningful and personalized to the two teachers' skills, the specific lesson, and the strengths and needs of the students.

Whole Class Structures

Whole class lessons emphasize cultivating relationships as a class community of learners. Each teacher has an active and

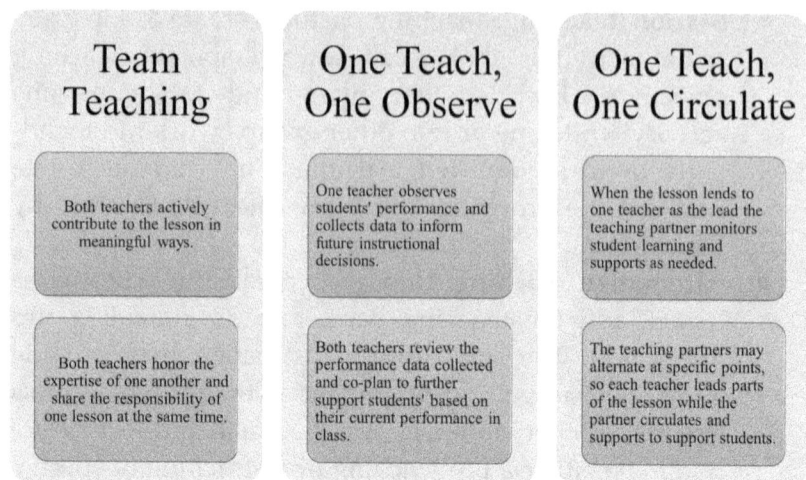

FIGURE 5.2 Whole Class Co-teaching Structures.

unique role based on their skills, expertise, and experiences. Both teachers work together to honor the contributions of one another while guiding an active learning process with their students (Stein, 2023). Teaching partners have the opportunity to provide students with varying perspectives and ramp up the learning by engaging students through the different qualities and personalities of both teachers (Stein, 2017). Figure 5.2 illustrates how to select the three models that empower the learners (including the two teachers) in any classroom.

Small Group Structures

Small group instruction works best when teachers are looking to increase students' active participation that may sometimes get lost in a whole class setting. Both teachers are actively available to directly work with individual students with a smaller teacher-student ratio. Each of the following co-teaching models also serve to close students' personal achievement gaps by learning skills and strategies they may apply in future whole class or small group instruction across time and settings. See Figure 5.3: Small Group Co-teaching Structures.

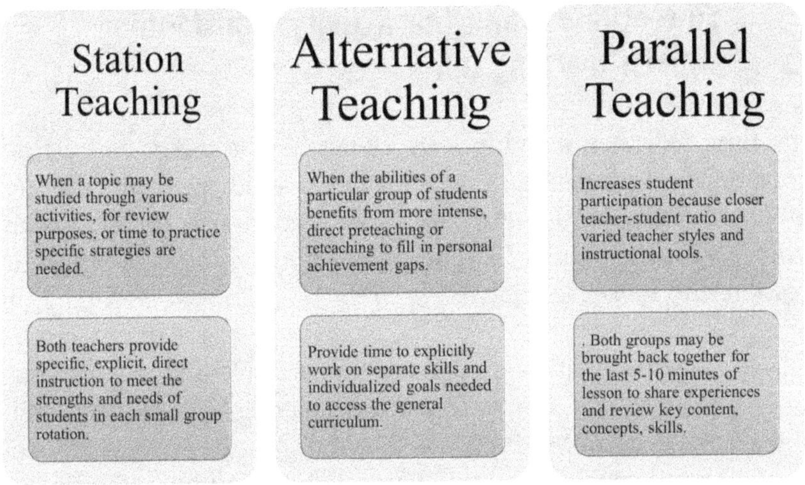

Station Teaching

When a topic may be studied through various activities, for review purposes, or time to practice specific strategies are needed.

Both teachers provide specific, explicit, direct instruction to meet the strengths and needs of students in each small group rotation.

Alternative Teaching

When the abilities of a particular group of students benefits from more intense, direct preteaching or reteaching to fill in personal achievement gaps.

Provide time to explicitly work on separate skills and individualized goals needed to access the general curriculum.

Parallel Teaching

Increases student participation because closer teacher-student ratio and varied teacher styles and instructional tools.

Both groups may be brought back together for the last 5-10 minutes of lesson to share experiences and review key content, concepts, skills.

FIGURE 5.3 Small Group Co-teaching Structures.

Key Takeaways

- ◆ Co-teaching models serve to structure co-teachers' collaborations and instructional flow for meaningful teaching and learning with students.
- ◆ The CPZ embraces the six most widely used models for effective co-teaching practices.
- ◆ Specific models support whole class or small group instruction.
- ◆ The co-teaching models optimize the active and meaningful participation of both teachers and all students.
- ◆ The CPZ supports individual co-teacher's contributions with a sense of being and awareness of their personal motivations, skills, and teaching abilities.
- ◆ The CPZ supports individual teachers entering into a sense of belonging with their co-teacher feeling empowered with a sense of being. Teaching within the co-teaching power zone provides the opportunity for co-teachers to embrace their own perspectives and expand their personal views by blending with their co-teaching partner's perspectives.
- ◆ The CPZ optimizes each co-teacher's personal power as they leverage their individual strengths and support one another to apply their strengths and continue to improve through meaningful collaborations.

Co-teaching Connection Activity: Transforming Your Co-teaching Self

It's time to check in with your co-teaching experience by first considering what is working and then extending your thinking and actions toward improving your experience for and with your co-teaching partner. Take a few minutes to jot down your response to these five sparks.

1. One think that is going well so far is…. (Thinking hints: consider which, if any, co-teaching models you are applying, what part of the day satisfies the three basic needs to feel competent, related and connected, and autonomous?)
2. What are one to three things that you are good at in your co-teaching role?
3. What is one skill or quality that you are contributing during the instructional moments?
4. What is one skill or quality that you want to contribute starting within the next day or so?
5. What is your co-teaching reality right now? What is your hope for your co-teaching experience as you commit to this ongoing process of learning and improvement?

Actions(s)/Interactions: What are two actions/interactions you can take to guide your transformative co-teaching journey this year? (Thinking Hints: What can YOU do? What would you like your co-teacher to do? Who else may you collaborate with to ignite your next action steps?)

Book Discussion Questions

1. Discuss the six co-teaching models. Specifically, how do you see them through the lens of supporting small group and whole class opportunities. How do the structures optimize co-teachers' and students' active and meaningful participation?
2. Why do you think it is important to vary the use of the co-teaching models? (Thinking hint: consider the aim to optimize meaningful and active participation from and with all learners—including the two teachers!).
3. Think of a recent or upcoming lesson. Which is the best model for you and your co-teacher to apply? Keep in mind, if you feel it is not working in the moments of instruction, you can switch to another model—right there in the natural flow of instruction in collaboration with your co-teacher and students.
4. In general, consider how the collaborations within the co-teaching models support each teacher's personal power. Think of a recent or upcoming lesson. How may your personal power be revealed? How may you support your co-teacher's personal power to blend with yours? How does this process empower students as learners alongside you and your co-teacher?

Now that you have completed all chapter readings, book discussion questions, and activities so far, it is time for one more activity, so you may earn your next puzzle piece! Are you ready? Great, let's go!

We Just Click! Co-teaching Character Action: Relate
Earn your Collaboration Jigsaw Puzzle Piece
Activity: Beyond Boundaries

Consider your experience with feeling competence, relatedness, and autonomy. Respond to the following questions by thinking about the routines, procedures, and daily responsibilities you and your co-teacher have set. Embrace where you are as your launching spot. Again, no judgment—just acknowledge it. Accept it. And be ready to move beyond boundaries!

Competence	What is one co-teaching model you applied within the last two weeks? How did the structure of the model help you to feel like a competent co-teacher? How did it make your co-teacher feel? What is one model you will try within the next two weeks to expand your co-teaching contributions? Discuss all the possibilities and then add one more model to your repertoire.
Relatedness	How do you and your co-teacher collaborate through a process of connecting, disconnecting, and reconnecting? What did you and your co-teacher do while you disconnected? Perhaps you took a yoga class, went on a nature walk, or read an article about a class-related topic? Perhaps it was that you felt more rested and balanced as the result of taking time for yourself. Maybe it was a specific strategy you learned after reading and researching. Share! And notice how the personal process of connecting, disconnecting, and reconnecting helps each of you to step into your individual and collective power! Talk about THAT!
Autonomy	Review your daily routine. At what point in the day do you feel like you are an active, willing participant? Do you feel you have a choice in how you participate? How can you and your co-teacher increase one another's sense of freedom during your co-teaching and learning routines?

We Just Click! Congratulations! It's time to celebrate! You earned your Collaboration Jigsaw puzzle piece. (Go to the Appendix, print out your puzzle piece, color it in or decorate it in any way your choice—cut it out and add it to the puzzle piece you already earned. Display in a prominent place for both of you to celebrate this accomplishment!)

Power
The Communication Zone

Chapter 6: Co-teaching in the Zone: Quick Check-In
Chapter 7: Incorporating Cogenerative Dialogues
Chapter 8: Using Story in Story (SiS) Approach to Expand Collaboration
Chapter 9: Tapping into Our Co-teaching Power with Discussion Tools
Chapter 10: Implementing Impactful Instructional Approaches for Co-teaching Power
Chapter 11: Applying Evidence-Based Practices Within the Co-teaching Power Zone

6

Co-teaching in the Zone
Quick Check-in

Here we are! We have reviewed the very human and very complex layers of any co-teaching process. The CPZ simplifies the complexity by reminding co-teachers that it is their personal relationship with one another that makes or breaks an effective co-teaching environment. Let's review the natural flow of co-teaching in the zone. Co-teaching in the zone begins with strengthening the roots for every co-teacher to increase their self-awareness within the motivation zone (see Part 1: Being). Through the important focus of self-awareness, each co-teacher then branches out into the collaboration zone (see Part 2: Belonging) where they come together to extend their individual perspectives in partnership. The process of connecting, disconnecting, and reconnecting empowers each individual. The motivation zone is always in the mix while branching out into the collaboration zone and strengthening the relationship of the teaching partners. The first two zones feed the roots of cultivating any co-teaching relationship. It honors, supports, and meets every co-teacher where they are in their co-teaching process. Each entry point of every co-teacher is the launching pad for creating personalized, respectful, and collaborative partnerships.

One of the core tenets of the CPZ is that each co-teacher must first belong to and with one another in partnership. This co-teaching relationship naturally permeates through the instructional process and the culture of the learning environment. As co-teachers flow through the zones, they reach their personalized degree of reciprocity. That is, each co-teacher feels a sense of autonomy, relatedness, and competence through transparent communication and a flow of connecting, disconnecting, and reconnecting with mutual respect. The co-teaching relationship creates a degree of reciprocity that then permeates through the instructional process where the students are brought into the process of collaboration. The co-teachers use dialogic practices to optimize the process of reciprocity with the students. Students have opportunities to, like the co-teachers, experience a sense of autonomy, relatedness, and competence. Students contribute to and with peers and the co-teachers along the learning process. The CPZ flows naturally with the co-teaching relationship and reciprocal instructional process into answering the question: *How does it feel to be a learner in this classroom?* The learning environment naturally becomes a comfortable, safe, supportive environment due to the mutual respect for honoring every perspective that comprises the collective voice of the unique group of learners in every class. The flow begins with the roots of the decision that two co-teachers make to cultivate their co-teaching relationship. These roots intertwine and branch out to welcome students into the growth fostering relationship with learning together. Figure 6.1 illustrates the way the CPZ flows when co-teachers commit themselves to experiencing teaching within the zone.

The CPZ embeds the power each co-teacher holds to inspire and be inspired by one another. When a co-teaching relationship results in a mutual sense of belonging, this relationship empowers the instructional process and learning environment and effectively impacts the ways all learners experience the process of learning in the classroom. Let's move along to learn specific tools co-teachers may apply to co-create meaningful and accessible instructional within a supportive learning environment.

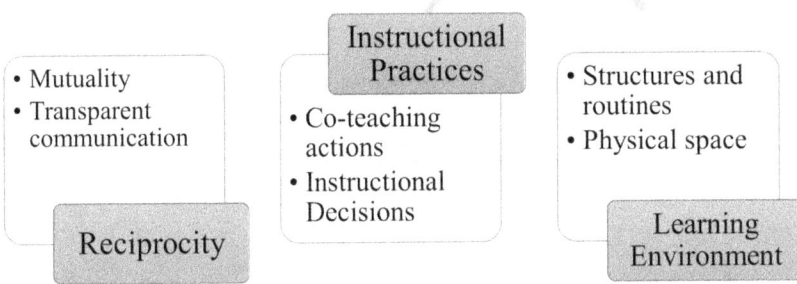

FIGURE 6.1 The Results of the CPZ Flow.

What are your personal takeaways so far? List 3–5 key ideas about the Co-teaching Power Zone Framework.

_____

_____

_____

_____

7
Incorporating Cogenerative Dialogues

A critical part of the communication zone and the co-teaching power zone (CPZ) is the evidence of ongoing transparent and reciprocal communication. Cogenerative dialogues (cogens) are active and interactive conversations in which learners gather to review their thoughts and ideas while sharing specific evidence to support their thinking. The purpose of cogenerative dialogues is to focus on the current culture of a classroom and the possible ways it may be transformed through the sharing of multiple perspectives. These liberating discussions ensure that members in the group feel valued as contributors to the conversation with the aim of working together to transform the classroom culture through embracing varied perspectives. In practice, these conversations may expose perceived roles of teachers and students with the classroom learning environment, which could lead to changes in the dynamics of power between teachers and students (Tobin, 2006; Stein, 2021, p. 40). My research found that cogens may also lead to changes in the dynamics of power between the co-teachers. Teachers agreed that through the cogen process, they "realized things that [they] may not have made time to think about" otherwise (Stein, 2021, p. 161). This chapter reviews how to implement cogenerative dialogues as a tool for increasing communication, strengthening co-teaching

DOI: 10.4324/9781003333692-11

relationships, and continue to improve co-teaching practices throughout the year (Stein, 2021).

According to Emdin (2010), cogenerative dialogues may expand teachers' awareness to seek new ways of teaching and then apply different methods as they apply students' feedback. Emdin further explains that this open communicative process has been shown to improve student motivation and engagement. The research on cogenerative dialogues reveal cogens as an effective tool for creating a learning environment where all learners—including the teachers—are actively involved, engaged, and valued as members of the classroom learning community (Elmesky & Tobin, 2005; Tobin & Roth, 2005; Bondi et al., 2016; Emdin, 2010; Stein, 2021, p. 41).

Cogen research began in response to educational reforms that promoted standards that challenged the complexities of race, ethnicities, gender, socioeconomics, and political concerns found in the process of teaching and learning of science in public schools (Elmesky & Tobin, 2005; Roth et al., 2002; Stein, 2021, p. 39).

My research (Stein, 2021) adds a new way of looking at applying cogenerative dialogues with two key points. First, cogenerative dialogues may be used to forge a stronger co-teaching partnership. In this way, cogens are applied between the co-teachers as a tool to expand perspectives as they strive to guide student learning. Although students may not be a part of the actual cogen process, teachers still include students' performance and evidence of classroom learning through anecdotal notes teachers create and student work samples to be analyzed. Second, I introduce cogens in a virtual learning process. Typically, cogens have been in person, with students. My research demonstrates the use of cogens with teachers with the option of virtual, synchronized discussions. My research expands the understanding that cogen between co-teachers in virtual or in-person experiences works to transform the culture of belonging and sense of community within the classroom. When the two teachers relate with one another first and foremost within the professional learning process, this sense of belonging permeates through their instructional decision and co-creation of their learning environment.

Getting Started with Cogenerative Dialogues

The critical first step here is to embrace where you and your co-teacher are at along the motivation to co-teach continuum. Remember, do not try to force any change here—just notice and embrace this personal entry point. This acceptance will allow you to work with how you feel now—not how you think you should be feeling. Consider this scenario:

> It is the day before school, an eager and enthusiastic special educator walks into the classroom to introduce herself to the general educator. "Hello, my name is Ms. H, and I am looking forward to working with you this year." "I know who you are" replied the general educator. "But I don't know what you are so excited about. I've co-taught many times before, and it just never worked—so why would this year be any different?"

The conversation above continued with the general educator sharing her past experiences. The special educator listened keenly. Although disappointed, the special educator was just thrilled at the way the general educator communicated her feelings and concerns. This scenario aligns seamlessly with the cogen process because both co-teachers were willing to engage in dialogue. Without dialogue, the general educator may have remained frustrated with co-teaching based on past experiences without even giving this new opportunity a chance.

Each cogen will be organically personalized simply due to the nature of unique personalities, experiences, and situations. However, there are some general procedures that may get any two co-teachers started as they develop their own communicative flow (see Figure 7.1).

The cogen process validates the feelings and thoughts of each co-teacher. The cogen process also optimizes opportunities for co-teachers to engage in transparent, reciprocal communication.

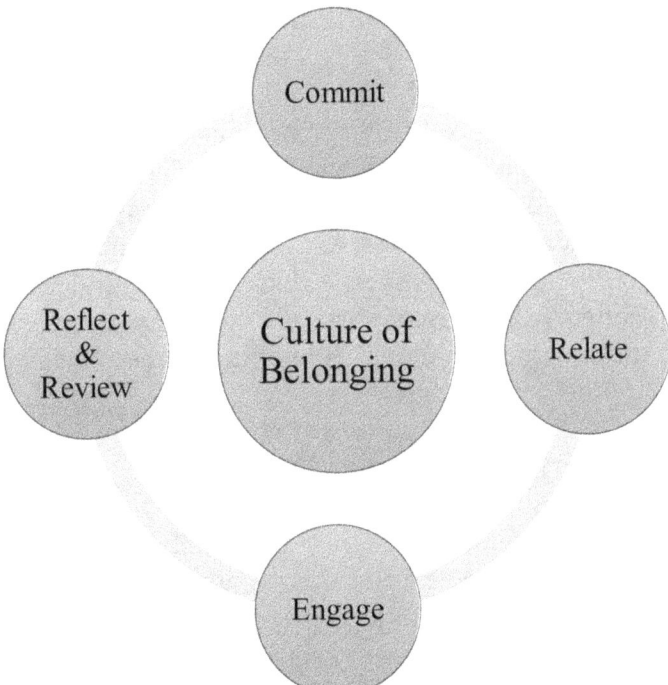

FIGURE 7.1 The General Cogenerative Dialogue Process.

General Process

1. **Commit**: Align your schedules to plan a cogen dialogue. Decide whether it is best for this session to be virtual or in person.
2. **Relate**: Decide on the topic for the cogen. If a specific topic is not needed, begin with an open-ended question, for example, *how are you doing with our co-teaching process?* Once the open dialogue has begun, be sure to listen to the perspective of your co-teacher and relate it to your thoughts and share.
3. **Engage**: Listen to one another actively. That means each co-teacher shares a complete thought without the other interrupting and vocally predicting what the other is saying. Speaking too quickly after the speaker shares a thought may also be considered an interruption. An instantaneous

response may indicate to the speaker that you weren't really listening and simply waiting for your turn to speak. The idea is to engage in active listening by staying focused on what your co-teacher is sharing, asking questions that extend their responses and your understanding of their ideas, and noticing non-verbal cues that may strengthen the communication process. Allow pauses when appropriate to let the silence increase reflection and thoughtful responses.
4. **Reflect & Review**: Expand and connect your co-teachers' ideas with your thoughts to optimize learning from one another's perspectives.

Examples to Consider
Example #1
Co-teacher A: I think things are going pretty well. I just wish that I was more active during class time. During class time, I have ideas for ways we could get more students to participate, but then the pace of the lesson keeps moving forward, and the moment is gone. (The teacher's shoulders sink a bit lower and their eyes gaze downward.)

Co-teacher B: (Sitting back in their chair, gazing at their motion of pushing a paperclip back and forth, the teacher responds.) I agree. I think things are going pretty well. I wish more kids would participate, too, but they are all involved in some way. We have so much content to cover in class that we just have to keep moving forward.

In the above example, co-teacher B acknowledges co-teacher A's general comment that things are going well. However, co-teacher B appears to avoid (or ignore) co-teacher A's real concern about student participation as evidenced by their comment and nonverbal cues (sinking shoulders and downward eye gaze). Co-teacher B glazed over Co-teacher A's concern and shifted to their own concern of feeling pressured to cover "so much content." Co-teacher A may not feel their thoughts are valued as evidenced by co-teacher B's oral response. Furthermore, co-teacher A may feel co-teacher B is disinterested as a result of co-teacher B's nonverbal cues of sitting back with visual focus on pushing a paperclip back and forth on the table.

Looking at figure 7.1, each co-teacher is committed to scheduling a cogen session, but barely touched upon other critical components of a meaningful cogenerative dialogue.

Let's take another look at this example and reimagine transparent, reciprocal communication.

Example #2

Co-teacher A: I think things are going pretty well. I just wish that I was more active during class time. During class time, I have ideas for ways we could get more students to participate, but then the pace of the lesson keeps moving forward, and the moment is gone. (The teacher shifts from sitting upright to sinking their shoulders a bit as their eyes gaze downward.)

Co-teacher B: (Stops pushing a paperclip back and forth and moves from sitting back in their chair to an upright position). I agree with you. Things are going well, and yet we can make things better. I hear you when you say the pacing of the lessons is fast. I do feel the pressure of teaching so much content in time for the students to get the information they need. Maybe there is a way to balance this out. What is one idea you have to increase student participation?

Co-teacher A: I have two ideas. Each of these ideas will not take time away from the time we need to work through the content. We can try one of the ideas this week and see how it goes. Which one do you want to try first?

In the example above, each co-teacher's concerns are expressed with a joint acknowledgment and effort to work on solutions—together. In this example, each of the critical components of a meaningful cogenerative dialogue was met. These two co-teachers naturally flowed through the commitment, relatedness, engagement, reflection, and review needed to keep improving upon their co-teaching practices. Furthermore, in alignment with the purpose of cogenerative dialogues, the pairing is clearly committed to transforming their culture of belonging by expressing their ideas, listening to one another's ideas, and expanding their own learning by embracing multiple perspectives.

Revisiting Three Basic Needs

Example #2 also illuminates the three basic needs we discussed in Part 1. Each co-teacher has the opportunity to

- Feel **autonomous** as each is willing to share and endorse their own actions. Co-teacher A also inserts an additional opportunity for co-teacher B to feel autonomous in this co-teaching experience by providing a choice in which strategy to try first.
- Feel a sense of **relatedness** where each is meaningfully contributing. Co-teacher A is contributing strategies to increase student participation. Co-teacher B is contributing the content lesson. Both co-teachers are sharing the responsibility to implement all aspects of the lesson.
- Feel a sense of **competence** as each co-teacher has the opportunity to plan and implement specific skills and areas of their pedagogical expertise.

Topics for Cogenerative Dialogues

The following are cogen scripts that may spark open dialogues to expand your co-teaching practices.

Cogenerative Dialogue Topic: Qualities of Effective Co-teachers
1. According to Freire (2018), open-mined educators exercise the following qualities: humility, courage, joy, decisiveness, and security.

- Which one quality do you feel is a strength for you?
- What is one way you applied this strength in a recent classroom lesson or activity?
- What is one quality you would like to work on to further strengthen your co-teaching skills?
- What is one example of how you may apply it in an upcoming lesson or activity?

Cogenerative Dialogue Topic: Motivation to Co-teach
1. Review Figure 2.1 in Chapter 2 and describe your motivation to co-teach. What is one way you may improve upon your motivation to commit to teaching and learning with your students and your teaching partner?
2. Look at Figure 2.2 in Chapter 2. Where do you live when considering your partnership reality? Explain. Where do you feel your co-teacher lives? Explain. Collectively, where do you live as a team?

Cogenerative Dialogue Topic: Three Basic Needs
1. Review the three basic human needs described in Chapter 1. Describe each need in general. How do you connect with each other? Be specific when describing evidence of whether each need is met or needs to be met from your perspective.
2. What is at least one thing you could do to improve the degree that your three basic needs are met in your co-teaching partnership?
3. What is at least one thing your co-teacher could do to support your three basic needs?
4. What is at least one thing you could do to support the development of your co-teacher's three basic needs?

Cogenerative Dialogue Topic: Collaboration along the CPZ
1. Consider the collaboration continuum in Chapter 4. Review Table 4.1. Where do you feel you and your co-teacher are performing at this point in time?
2. What can you do to improve your collaborative relationship with your co-teacher?
3. What is one thing you would like your co-teacher to do to support collaboration moving toward sustained or increased reciprocity?

Transformative Possibilities
Ongoing cogenerative dialogues create opportunities for co-teachers to work through ideas and situations that may otherwise drive a wedge between the two teachers. Co-teachers

strengthen and continue to improve their practice as a result of the following cogenerative dialogue agreements:

- Each co-teacher connects with their perspective
- Co-teachers expand their learning by learning from and with their co-teacher's perspective
- Each co-teacher increases their awareness of how they are experiencing the three basic needs of humans to be effective in social contexts.
- Each co-teacher expands their awareness for how their co-teacher is experiencing the three basic needs.
- As co-teachers listen to one another, together, they decide on ways they may adjust their actions.

Throughout this book be sure to notice other topic ideas for cogenerative dialogues. The next chapter reviews a tool I call the Story in Story (SiS) approach (Stein, 2021, 2023). This is another practical tool that may guide co-teachers to expand their understanding of the complexities of co-teaching by embracing multiple perspectives. The SiS approach is also an effective and simple tool to use to guide co-teachers to negotiate the power and expertise of both teachers in the room.

Cogenerative Dialogue Topic: Deeper Collaboration by the Process of Connecting, Disconnecting, and Re-connecting

1. Share one example of how you and your co-teacher connect. How may this continue or be improved?
2. What is one area where you need time to explore or plan on your own as you consider an upcoming lesson or activity?
3. What is one area your co-teacher needs time to plan or explore on their own?
4. Are you both open to coming back together to share and synthesize your ideas? If so, celebrate by expressing your gratitude with one another. If not, celebrate that as well by acknowledging the current access point. Making time to discuss is the first step. Utilizing the dialogic time meaningfully may need a little more time to establish the

relationship. Keep meeting and consider going back to a cogenerative dialogue topic discussed at the end of Part 1 to build a better foundation as you move toward transparent, reciprocal conversations and actions.

Virtual Cogenerative Dialogues

As mentioned earlier in this chapter, the research on cogenerative dialogues reveals ways for students and teachers to reflect on class procedures, events, and lessons and then work collaboratively with the aim of improving the teaching and learning process. The CPZ Framework introduces two new ideas for applying cogenerative dialogues. First, the use of cogens is shared as a powerful tool that may guide two teachers to continuously improve their co-teaching practices through dialogue. Second, cogenerative dialogues may be extended beyond the physical classroom into virtual spaces. The CPZ Framework incorporates the notion that creating the classroom culture is not bound to the physical space in the classroom. Classroom culture may also exist in the wide-open synchronous and asynchronous spaces that bring students and teachers together (Stein, 2021, p. 161). Virtual cogenerative dialogues may empower co-teachers in a number of ways. First, it responds to time management restraints to allow for thoughtful dialogue outside of the school day. Second, it may further strengthen relationships between the two co-teachers because they are continuing to problem-solve and brainstorm ideas outside of the routine schedule of a typical school day. Finally, it can bring teachers closer together because they have the opportunity to naturally share aspects of their personal life, perhaps their pets, family members, and hobbies will make their way into the conversations. Teachers who virtual cogenerative dialogues reported looking forward to their time together, feeling like part of each other's family, and noticing they became more open to thinking about new ways of teaching and learning because they were learning from and with one another (Stein, 2021). The use of online tools to communicate in virtual spaces filters our lens to see beyond how the typical view of co-teaching collaborations flows. Opportunities to meet during synchronous video calls such as Zoom, Google Meets, and even FaceTime, to name a few, can transcend a typical process of communication in physical classrooms.

Furthermore, The CPZ Framework honors the time for teachers to connect, disconnect, and reconnect as an organic and powerful way to meaningfully collaborate. The use of Google Docs, email, and other asynchronous tools serve to empower each teacher as they tend to their own personal and professional growth before coming back together to apply their personal contributions and expertise during cogen sessions and within the process of teaching and learning in the classroom.

Key Takeaways

- ♦ The communication zone within the CPZ is about experiencing and creating evidence of ongoing, transformative, and reciprocal communication between co-teachers.
- ♦ Cogenerative dialogues (aka cogens) are active conversations that provide opportunities for co-teachers to articulate their perspectives and share with one another for expanded awareness around a selected topic/situation.
- ♦ The purpose of cogenerative dialogues is to focus on the current co-teaching culture in the classroom and consider possible ways to transform and improve co-teaching practices by sharing multiple perspectives.
- ♦ The general four-step process of engaging in cogenerative dialogues is first to schedule and commit to an agreed-upon time. The second step is to agree upon a topic that needs to be shared. The third step is to engage in conversation by listening and speaking actively and compassionately to and with one another. The final step is to review key points of the conversation and reflect on possible next steps to ensure both co-teachers walk away with a shared understanding.
- ♦ The cogenerative dialogues serve to support and illuminate the three basic human needs, so each co-teacher

has the opportunity to evolve with feelings of autonomy, relatedness, and competence.
- The CPZ introduces the notion of virtual cogenerative dialogues. To expand possibilities around time management, co-teachers have the option to engage in these conversations in person or at another agreed-upon time synchronously via digital methods such as Zoom, Google Meet, and FaceTime.
- Virtual cogenerative dialogues have been proven to be successful in guiding co-teachers to become more aware of their current classroom culture, co-teaching practices, and the ways they may work together to improve and transform their culture over time (Stein, 2021).

Co-teaching Connection Activity: Express Yourself! Keeping a Solution-Seeking Mindset through Teamwork

Consider your thoughts! Your thoughts are powerful ways to increase communication with yourself and your co-teacher. For every expression on the left, consider the solution on the right as you reframe your thinking to focus on possible solutions for healthy, transparent co-teaching collaborations!

Expression	Possible solutions
It makes me feel…when you…	How about we try….
At times you seem to…and I feel…	How does that make you feel?
How can we improve upon…	What ways may we support one another as we work together to connect students with this lesson (or overall learning in the classroom)?
(Add your expression here—what's on your mind?)	(Add a possible solution based on your expression here—brainstorm with your co-teacher.)

Book Discussion Questions

1. Explain how the process of cogenerative dialogues could empower you as a co-teacher. What specific topic would be a desired topic for you and your co-teacher? (Thinking hint: consider how things are going. Is there something that you would like to contribute to or something you would like to see changed? Perhaps you would just like to discuss what is going well—that is always a good place to start!).
2. Consider how your actions (or non-actions) affect your co-teacher's actions. Also, how do your co-teacher's actions (or non-actions) affect the way you perform in the classroom? How do you support (or not support) one another? If you have time, have a quick cogen to discuss this question, and then see how your actions and interactions transform right before your eyes!
3. Review the examples of cogenerative topics shared in this chapter. Which one most resonates with you and why? Be sure to share with your co-teacher and hear what they have to say resonates with them as well.
4. Consider the power of in-person and synchronous virtual cogenerative dialogues. Discuss the benefits of each. Be specific.

8
Using Story in Story (SiS) Approach to Expand Collaboration

When needing to work in partnership, it is so easy to get lost in the cycle of thought around our own perspectives that in turn create our reality for any given situation. Comments like "I can't believe he did that" or "I just don't feel welcome in the classroom" are examples of a co-teacher who has a keen focus on their perspective that then unfolds into their actions toward feeding into those beliefs. Due to holding on to one's personal perspective, these actions may be a co-teacher who acts as a "guide on the side" who may be frustrated by not feeling like an active participant. However, if we commit to expanding our perspective to include our co-teacher's perspective, we can clear the path toward reciprocal co-teaching actions. For example, "My co-teacher is concerned about time management, so we carefully inserted moments when students apply what we are teaching" or "I felt so frustrated, but then once I shared my thoughts, my co-teacher was open to applying the strategy." Comments such as these expand co-teaching practices. Yet, the human condition does not always make it easy for us to expand our perspectives. Individuals naturally get caught in the comfort of their own view. Enter the Story in Story (SiS) approach. This dialogic tool increases reciprocal and transparent communication between co-teachers. The approach makes the thoughts of each co-teacher visible as a means of increasing understanding and expediting effective co-teaching practices. The SiS approach works to cultivate growth-fostering relationships that effectively permeate through the instructional practices and co-creation of the learning environment. It also serves as a proactive measure to respond to any natural need for conflict resolutions. It is also a successful tool for administrators to use to support autonomous co-teaching pairings (Stein, 2023). Let's take a look at how the SiS approach flows within the continuum of the power zone and CPZ by relaxing with a few examples of co-teaching experiences.

It's time to illuminate the many perspectives that blend into one effective co-teaching experience. Think about it. First, there's the perspective of each co-teacher and every student in their class. Posing the question: "How is co-teaching going in your class?" would reveal a variety of different responses. Principals and other administrators, parents and other stakeholders are also perspectives that influence co-teachers' decisions.

SiS #1: It's All the Little Things

It was the end of the year, and I was asked to meet with a group of "disgruntled" educators. The principal told me he tried everything, and he just wants to be proactive, so they do not have another year like the one they just had. "We just have to get this co-teaching thing right," he pleaded. Ms. Lacey was one of seven co-teachers who were experiencing significant frustrations in their efforts to meet the varying demands of their co-teaching schedules. In addition, they posed their shared reality of additional daily disappointments. The principal and I decided to organize a team meeting to address their thoughts. We met in a large conference room. The principal of this high school, seven special educators, and eight general educators were present.

Ms. Lacey was the first to speak. She co-taught with four different general educators. As the special educator, she made time each week to meet with each teacher to get the plans for the following week, so she could prepare the ways she would support students' learning. Her efforts to co-plan resulted in each teacher sending her digital links or a quick email to the content of the lessons ahead. On occasions the co-teachers were able to co-plan during their prep periods, Ms. Lacey was exhausted by chasing her time (and energy) to meet with four different teachers while still maintaining her busy teaching day—including providing extra help to the students during lunch. "Even when we plan, and I think I am prepared, the lesson is different from what they told me when I walk into class anyway." Ms. Lacey understands the pace and the need to go with the flow, so she works each night to plan for "just in case" kinds of strategies that may be needed. She shared her frustration with her "inhuman and unnecessary" amount of overplanning. As this organic conversation flowed, I took notes. Using their words, I created the SiS map below: SiS #1: It's all the little things.

SiS Summary #1: The meeting took about 30 minutes. I facilitated comments and questions—such as "Who would like to add their thoughts? Thank you for sharing" and "How is it going for you" as I acknowledged everyone in the room. They were invited to share—not expected to share. The greatest takeaways were the special educators who raised awareness for "all the little things" that when blended together on a daily, weekly, and yearly basis add up to many challenges in creating equitable and autonomous co-teaching experiences. Solutions were discussed such as using digital shared documents for planning. Also, the principal gained and expanded perspective as co-teachers shared that just keeping co-teachers together isn't always the best choice. Sometimes change is necessary.

SiS #1: It's All the Little Things

Special Educators

- Need consistent co-planning.
- Need open communication to discuss plans as they change.
- Want our name on report cards, classroom doors, and anywhere a teacher's name is supposed to be.
- Would be nice to consider pairings that really work and not just keep teachers together for convenience.
- Things are going well enough—it's just all the little things.

General Educators

- We can keep a digital document of our plans, so changes can be seen in real time.
- We thought everything was going okay. We didn't realize how much juggling you have.
- We can get so caught up in the content and the pressure of time; it is hard to balance meeting the needs of all students.
- It's true; sometimes a change in co-teaching is needed.

Principal

- I can make sure that co-planning time is embedded in the day.
- I thought keeping co-teachers together was a good thing! We can check in with all of you more often before making new pairings.
- We can work on getting your names in the system—that just makes good sense—you're right.

SiS Summary #2: She Just Takes All the Energy of the Room

Ms. Jouldan and Ms. Therian were together for English and science class. Ms. Jouldan was new to teaching in this middle school and Ms. Therian was a special educator in the district for ten years. Both shared a willingness to co-teach and work together. Yet, it was known across the grade level that they were not getting along. Ms. Therian was heard telling someone she was counting down the days of this frustrating year. Of course, it got back to Ms. Jouldan who replied: "I hear that! I feel the same way. Working with her is not easy. She just takes all the energy out of the room." Although both teachers were frustrated, they were reminded that they did want to co-teach and work together earlier in the year. They decided to give the SiS approach a go. Each teacher had an index card and wrote down their main thoughts on their current situation. They placed their cards on the table, so it was clearly visible as they discussed.

SiS #2: It Just Takes All the Energy in the Room

Special Educator

- Co-planning is disorganized.
- Every lesson feels too unstructured without a clear direction.
- Enjoy the way they relate to the students together as a team.

General Educator

- A little overwhelmed learning the new curriculum.
- Feels confused with the best way to structure lessons in a way that is good for all of the students.
- Gets frustrated when Ms. Therian makes decisions for how to teach in the moments because it forces the pacing to slow down too much for many of the students.

The takeaways that resulted from this SiS exercise for these two co-teachers were the following:

Ms. Therian had no idea that she was being "bossy" or overstepping her power by making instructional decisions in the moments. "I was just so focused on meeting the needs of so many students." She also didn't realize that Ms. Jouldan was overwhelmed with learning the curriculum. "I just thought you were disorganized and not savvy with ways to teach—so I just jumped in with frustration." Both teachers realized they needed to communicate better and made a commitment to "work out the kinks" together.

The SiS approach opens lines of communication that allow for multiple paths of power to meet. All views are shared, valued, and solutions and productive interactions unfold as a result. As we consider the many co-teaching stories that exist—the SiS approach provides an opportunity for everyone to tell their story, honor the stories of others, and work together toward effective solutions and interactions. Furthermore, the SiS approach was created to guide educators to become more keenly aware of their personal co-teaching assumptions as they share and learn with others through this expanding perspective process.

Key Takeaways

- ♦ The CPZ introduces the SiS approach that serves as a dialogic tool for embracing the experiences of both co-teachers within the communication zone.
- ♦ The SiS approach is a dialogic tool that increases reciprocal and transparent communication by illuminating each co-teacher's perspective in audible and visual ways.
- ♦ The SiS approach is an organic process that cultivates growth-fostering relationships through accessible, meaningful, and authentic dialogue.
- ♦ Through the SiS process, each co-teacher's perspective is valued, each voice is heard, and every story is told. Perspectives are then discussed toward reaching solutions for effective, respectful, and meaningful co-teaching practices.

Co-teaching Connection Activity: Four "A"s Text Protocol

(adapted from School Reform Initiative): This activity guides co-teachers to explore their personal values and beliefs about co-teaching as they expand their perspective by learning from and with their co-teacher's views.

Process: Each co-teacher independently considers their knowledge and beliefs about co-teaching from their own experiences so far and then responds to the following questions in dialogue with their co-teacher.

1. What **Assumptions** do you have about co-teaching? (What are your expectations, beliefs about its effectiveness, and ideas about the process, etc.?)
2. What co-teaching belief do you **Agree** with your co-teacher about?
3. What do you want to **Argue** (constructively) with your co-teacher about?
4. What is it about co-teaching in your current partnership that you want to **Aspire** to do or **Act** upon to continue to improve the flow of learning in your classroom?

Bringing it all together! Following the discussion above, conclude the conversation by each responding to this question: What do our responses mean for our collaborative work as a teaching team? What does it mean for our impact on student learning?

Book Discussion Questions

1. Summarize the process of the SiS approach, and then share what you find most valuable about the process. What do you find most challenging? What is at least one possible solution to your identified challenge?
2. Think of a recent or upcoming lesson, classroom situation, or scenario. What is your perspective? What is your co-teacher's perspective? How could blending both perspectives empower your students to meaningfully participate?
3. This chapter shares examples of the SiS approach in action. Share which scenario you connect with and explain why.
4. Finish this sentence: I am excited to try the SiS approach because….

We Just Click! Co-teaching Characteristic Action: Communicate:

Earn your Connect Jigsaw Puzzle Piece (1 piece—indicates that each co-teacher feels heard—shared perspectives—in some way…. Each writes word/speaks/sketches…how feel connected—"I am heard" I am ready, I am open, I am learning, etc.…)

After completing the chapter reading, book club questions, and activities so far, you are ready to earn a co-teaching communication jigsaw puzzle piece!

Perspective Pioneer: For each word listed, each co-teacher should create a response to express how they connect with each word. Be ready to share and engage in an ongoing growth fostering relationship!

What makes you feel…
1. unique? _____   5. challenged? _____
2. excited? _____   6. confused? _____
3. inspired? _____   7. human? _____
4. balanced? _____   8. liberated in the classroom? _____

We Just Click! Congratulations! It is time to celebrate! You earned your Connect Jigsaw puzzle piece! After the two of you share your perspective pioneer responses and understand your own perspective and the perspective of the other, make a copy of the Connect puzzle piece in the Appendix, color it in or decorate it, and display in a prominent place that is a visual reminder of co-teaching pride for each of you each day.

9
Tapping into Our Co-teaching Power with Discussion Tools

Earlier in the book, co-teaching power was defined as the ways the co-teachers leverage their individual strengths and abilities and honor the strengths and abilities of one another. Within this process, each co-teacher organically supports the growth of one another as they work in an energizing feedback loop that allows each to learn and improve individually and together. Applying the idea that our own power impacts others (Hawkins, 2014), each co-teacher has the opportunity to expand their perspective and their overall co-teaching experience by being impacted by their teaching partner (Stein, 2023). This transformative co-teaching process is at the heart of the CPZ. With consciousness, intention, and discernment, each co-teacher can find their personal co-teaching truth and co-create a fulfilling, meaningful inclusive experience for and with each other and their students.

The communication zone and the flow of the Co-teaching Power Zone (CPZ) Framework remind teachers that power is a natural and encouraging part of the human experience, and specifically applied to guide meaningful and sustainable co-teaching partnerships. Within the CPZ, power exists in effective ways when each co-teacher learns from and with

DOI: 10.4324/9781003333692-13

the other through dialogue and through the freedom for each to act in ways that effectively impact the learning process for teachers and students. The communication zone tools and the CPZ Framework serve as a solid structure that can empower each co-teacher and to raise awareness with both teachers, as a partnership, to feel the power within themselves and within their collective strengths and abilities—as a team to reach their best possible co-teaching experience. The CPZ embraces that the power of one co-teacher to act in their role as an educator is generally for social good. However, co-teachers need to distinguish between *power to do and to act* and *power over others* (Fairclough, 2015). Fairclough guides individuals to become aware of the ways we use our own power. He reminds us that we need to see this power distinction in dialectical ways. He states, "...having power over people increases power to do things; power to do things is conditional (in some cases at least) on having power over people" (p. 26). There are situations in society where power over others can be a good thing—such as an elected official, a doctor, or teacher who has legitimate power over us. However, there are times when power over others is not legitimate and results in conflicts, frustrations, possible negative effects to well-being (p. 27). The CPZ includes a guided framework and tools that support co-teachers with a *power to* work together in harmony—to negotiate their power— and to honor the well-being of themselves and each other. The CPZ eliminates any possibility for *power over* to enter the co-teaching process. Within the CPZ, the natural movement between the co-teachers creates opportunities for co-teachers to embrace their own motivations and sense of purpose in their co-teaching role. This heightened awareness provides the space for one co-teacher to begin to see and to address how their thoughts and actions affect their co-teaching partner's actions. Through dialogic methods, specifically cogenerative dialogues, the co-teachers begin to express their perspectives providing the opportunity for each co-teacher to expand their own understanding and to improve their co-teaching experience together. One teacher does not have the power over the

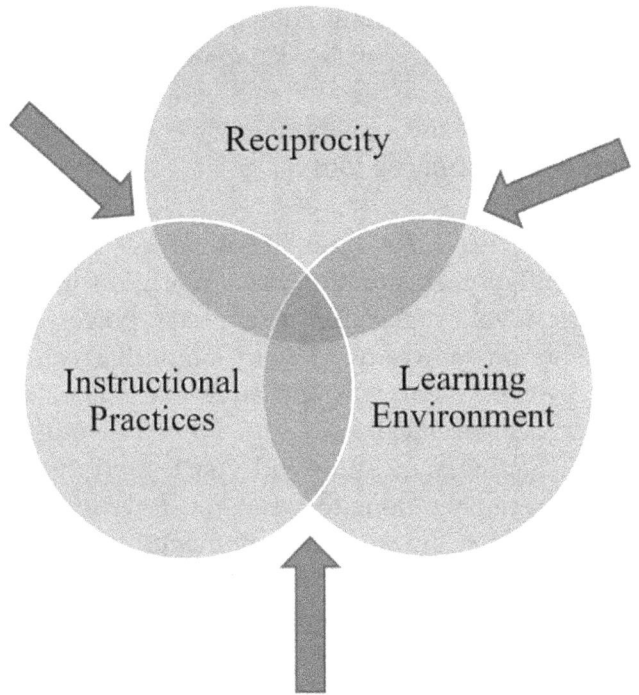

FIGURE 9.1 Co-powered Experiences within the CPZ.

other. They each come with the power to participate with mutual understanding. Collaboration is embraced as a continuum where there is the natural need to connect, disconnect, and reconnect to further empower and improve their co-teaching relationship with effective impacts on their instructional decisions and culture within their learning environment. Figure 9.1, Co-powered experiences within the CPZ, shows the three interrelated fields come together through cogenerative dialogues and by honoring one another through the natural flow of connecting, disconnecting, and reconnecting (noted by the arrows pointing to the overlapping fields).

The following Co-teacher Power Analysis Tool may be used to guide you and your co-teachers to check-in with how the basics of power is experienced between the two of you. In the spirit of critical pedagogy and the decades of research that is interlaced within the CPZ, be as transparent as possible. Once the tool is completed, make sure to share your perspectives at your next cogenerative dialogue session (see Chapter 7).

Co-teacher Power Analysis Tool

1. Think about three different situations with your co-teacher. For each situation put a mark to show whether you felt your co-teacher exercised "power to" work together or "power over" you—hindering your actions. Be specific. What was the situation? What did your co-teacher specifically say and do? As a result of your co-teacher's actions, how did you feel and why? What could have been done to make you feel different? What could be done to keep the momentum of partnership between you both going? What can you both do to keep improving your co-teaching experience? (Figure 9.2)

As we begin to identify our legitimate, unique, and authentic use of power as co-teachers, we must be consistently mindful of our choice to exert power to work harmoniously together. When co-teachers work in harmony, they consistently negotiate power by leveraging and honoring their own strengths and abilities as well as their co-teaching partner's strengths and abilities. In this flow of actions and interactions, each co-teacher will learn from and with each other to transform their current co-teaching experience. The CPZ also emphasizes the power of language as an effective tool for always improving our teaching partnerships. The language we use first enters the scene with our personal thoughts. Our thoughts become our actions. Our actions affect the actions of others. The next section reviews possible ways to shift our language from building walls to co-creating open spaces of co-teaching freedom and partnerships.

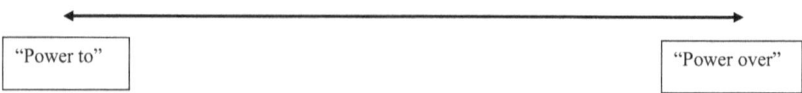

FIGURE 9.2 Co-teacher Power Analysis Tool.

Using Discourse Analysis to Move from Walls to Open Spaces

We have all heard the realistic statement that teachers make countless decisions each day. Within any given day of making countless decisions, the language we use to communicate can go easily unnoticed. Yet, that is not entirely true because the language others use to communicate can easily be *felt* and then tossed aside because we go back into the busy mode of making countess decisions each day. Yet, if tossed aside one too many times, the pile of tossed aside feelings can easily become walls. Once these invisible—but keenly felt—walls are created, communication breaks down, and it is often hard to get back. So, let's consider how we can knock down walls that may become a wedge between co-teachers. Even better—let's consider not building these walls at all! Let's be intentional with our language—or at least become more aware of how our language is contributing to our co-teaching relationships. Let's discuss a discourse analysis tool to help us to naturally go from walls to open spaces where communication and co-teaching relationships may flow freely and productively.

What Is Critical Discourse Analysis?

Along with the CPZ, discourse analysis refers to our ability to analyze and shift our language in ways that honor the strengths, abilities, and humanity of each co-teacher. Gee (2014) explains that analyzing language (a.k.a critical discourse analysis (CDA) is a set of tools that allow us to make sense of how the language we use relates to our actions. That is, let's not just think of language as something said, written, or gestured and then toss it aside for invisible, but powerful walls to be created. No! There are ways to organically increase our awareness of how language may easily promote co-teaching power. Specifically, we will look at how our language and the language of our co-teacher has a direct connection with our co-teaching actions and classroom experiences.

> Language has a magical property: when we speak or write, we design what we have to say to fit the situation in which we are communicating. But at the same

time, how we speak or write creates that very situation. It seems then, that we fit our language to a situation that our language, in turn, helps to create in the first place.

(Gee, 2005 p. 10)

Gee (2014) guides an understanding of how we can analyze our language in ways that guide our actions. He outlines three important connections along the function and flow of language.

Figure 9.3 shares the effects of that language. The basic flow of language connects how the language flows into our actions and ultimately into our how we perceive ourselves in the context of the situation we are communicating.

It is important to note that actions refer to a deeper meaning beyond mere "speech acts" where someone merely provides a verbal response. Actions can also be gestures that do not require verbal response. Everything that is said connects with some form of action that leads to the human experience of feeling a certain way and connecting with our own identities. Let's move to specific tools that may be applied to further explain how CDA may be used to move from walls to open spaces of effective, communicative co-teaching experiences.

Use Table 9.1 to guide you to use CDA tools to empower your co-teaching collaborations.

Why use these tools?

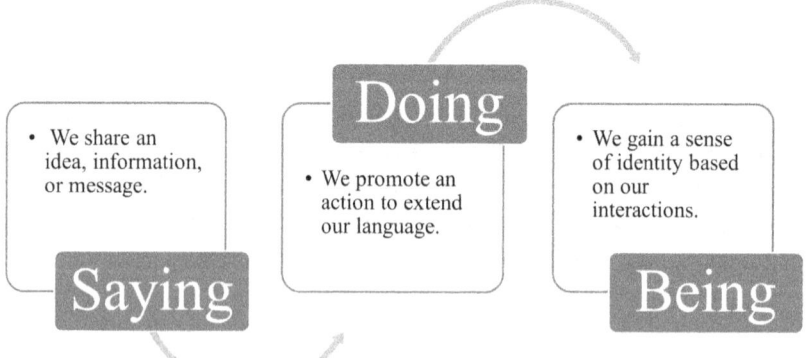

FIGURE 9.3 The Flow of Language: Saying, Doing, Being.

TABLE 9.1 CDA tools to empower your co-teaching collaborations

Discussion tool	How to use	How it strengthens communication between co-teachers
The Fill-in Tool	Based on the context of the conversation or situation and what was said between the co-teachers, what may be filled in to provide further clarity. What may be inferred by the message of the discussion even if it wasn't overtly stated.	Expands communication by thinking beyond what was said, heard, and felt at the surface level. Builds deeper understanding by considering.
The Making Strange Tool	Take a step away from the conversation or situation. Pretend that you are observing two co-teachers that you do not know (they are strangers). They are experiencing the same situation you are currently having. What advice would you give them toward effective solutions and communication? Another way to use this tool is to take a step away from your conversation or situation with your colleague. Be an outside observer of what is going on. Objectively notice what knowledge or assumptions are occurring. This objective view may shine a light on ways you may address any needed aspects of the conversation or situation.	Broadens perspective and deescalates emotions that may interfere with productive communication. Guides co-teachers to not take something in a personal way and illuminates the necessary focus to keep communication flowing productively.
The Frame Tool	Consider the context of the conversation. Just when you think you have all the information you need, ask yourself: *Is there anything else I need to know to provide more details about the context of the conversation or situation?* Always push your knowledge of the context surrounding your conversation further to see if other relevant information may provide further clarity for effective communication.	Ensures that all the necessary information is considered and expressed.

(Continued)

TABLE 9.1 (Continued)

Discussion tool	How to use	How it strengthens communication between co-teachers
The Why This Way to Add to That Way Tool	Each co-teacher asks themselves why their teaching partner expressed themselves in the way they did and not some other way. Consider how the co-teacher may value the intentions of their co-teaching partner—and add their ideas to expand and broaden teaching and learning opportunities.	Considers the perspective of your co-teaching partner. May minimize frustration as the intentions of your teaching partner are understood. Also, opens the conversation for you to share your perspective and another way of saying or doing something within the context of your teaching situation.
The Context is Reflexive Tool	Each co-teacher reflects and discusses the following questions: 1. How is what my co-teaching partner is saying and how they are saying it creating, shaping (or possibly manipulating) my own actions? 2. How is what my co-teaching partner is saying and doing supporting our teaching partnership in a given lesson or situation? 3. Is what my co-teaching is saying and doing helping to maintain a status quo or working to transform and improve our co-teaching practices?	Expands a focus on valuing the ideas and actions of each co-teacher. May guide a shift from teaching solo to sharing the responsibility of all phases of the instructional process. Furthermore, this tool emphasizes ongoing growth and improvement as two teachers experience a growth-fostering co-teaching experience.
The Significance Building Tool	Each co-teacher asks how their words and actions build up or lessen the importance of their teaching partner's role. In addition, co-teachers may use this tool to decide how they build up or lesson the relevance for certain teaching practices and not others.	Supports the value of two active co-teachers by each considering the way(s) they may team up with their teaching partner's expertise.

(Continued)

TABLE 9.1 (Continued)

Discussion tool	How to use	How it strengthens communication between co-teachers
The Activities Building Tool	What specific instructional practice is this communication building or enacting? What activities are being enacted based on what is being said or done? How is each co-teacher supporting one another as an active contributor along the instructional process? How is each co-teacher meaningfully interacting with students?	Emphasizes each co-teacher's part in either implementing or not implementing certain co-teaching practices. Shines a light on specific co-teaching models or instructional strategies that would optimize learning for students while both co-teachers are meaningfully active (autonomous).
The Doing and Not Saying Tool	Consider a strong focus on the actions of each co-teacher. Hear what they are saying and try to keenly notice what they are trying to do to fully understand and work together. 1. Does my co-teacher's words match their actions? 2. How do your co-teacher's actions inform your own ways of communicating?	Expands perspectives and understanding by noticing different ways we communicate. This tool reminds us to remember the old adage "Actions speak louder than words."
The Identities Building Tool	What role or identity is the co-teacher trying to enact or get their co-teacher to recognize? How does one co-teacher position the other co-teacher? How does each co-teacher contribute to the identity of their teaching partner?	Builds reciprocity and trust by being aware of the way each co-teacher contributes to how their teaching partner's role takes shape.
The Connections Building Tool	How does the language of one co-teacher connect or disconnect with their co-teaching partner? Does one co-teacher ignore key ideas or feelings that are relevant to their teaching partner?	Guides each co-teacher to consider whether what they say and do builds or lessens connection with their teaching partner. Specific solutions for building connections may be discussed and acted upon as a result of considering using this tool.

These helpful tools work to guide co-teachers to look deeper and better understand the intentions of one another. Gee's CDA tools have been adapted for organic collaboration within the CPZ.

Let's consider a few scenarios with one possible example of applying a CDA tool for each scenario. Please let your imagination run wild and consider another tool as a solution for each scenario.

Examples of CDA in Action along the CPZ

Through lens of CDA, the purpose of language moves beyond simply sharing information. We must also be aware of the complex relationship between language and action (Gee, 2014). This section shares specific co-teaching scenarios along with possible CDA tools as solutions for creating a clear and productive path of communication between co-teachers. These tools may be used during cogenerative dialogues as teachers come together to meaningfully collaborate along the CPZ process.

Scenario #1: Stop Stealing My Thunder?!

Context: Two co-teachers are in a high school social studies class. The general educator is at the front of the class explaining visual images on slides as the special educator circulates around the room keenly noticing how the students are responding to the lesson. The special educator wished to add additional examples to further guide students' understanding, but the opportunity does not arise. The general educator moves through the slides providing explanations for each. From past conversations, the special educator understands that the general educator does not want to be interrupted during any lesson. However, the special educator feels frustrated because she knows that students are required to take notes; yet, as usual, she sees many blank pages in students' notebooks. She decides to model notetaking to guide students' attention and skill of notetaking. She quietly stood at the side of the room and began to write notes on a sideboard based on key ideas shared by the general educator. The special educator noticed five students sit up from their slouched positions to begin writing in their notebooks. She felt a sense of relief to know that students were being provided with additional support to guide more active learning. Although hesitant to model notetaking because she and the co-teacher did not discuss first, she felt confident because she was not interrupting her co-teacher's lesson. She was quietly supporting it—or so she thought. After three minutes of modeling the notes, the general educator stopped talking and looked at the special educator and said, "What are you doing—you are stealing my thunder."

Consider These Questions for Discussion:
1. How would you describe the co-teachers' communication patterns? How do you know?
2. What co-teaching model was being applied?
3. What could each co-teacher do to expand their communication—while honoring one another's strengths, abilities, and power?

CDA Tool: The Identity Building Tool
This tool illuminates how language provides the power for an individual to be recognized as having a certain identity or role. We act out different identities as we live within different contexts. For example, one special educator may be co-teaching with a variety of general educators. The same general educator may easily experience a different identity depending on the co-teacher they are teaching with and the subject area they are teaching. Furthermore, each co-teacher comes with different areas of expertise and experiences. What are the patterns in their ways of expressing their sense of who they are as co-teachers? According to Gee (2014), people use language to create different identities for themselves in different contexts. Furthermore, people can also help others to create their sense of identity. In the case of scenario #1, the general educator used language as a way to create the identity as the lead teacher. All of his language and actions supported the special educator to gain the view of their identity as a quiet,

passive member of the teaching team. The special educator however attempted to create an identity as an active contributor to the learning process. She honored the general educator's wish for her to remain quiet. However, when her nonverbal—but visual—language via modeling notetaking unfolded, the general educator could not accept this change in the special educator's identity. There are clear tensions and contradictions between the way the special and general educator build the special educator's identity. However, do you notice that both the general and special educator build the general educator's role as lead teacher—with the special educator's role as remaining passive and quiet? Let's look at the general process for applying the identity building tool in your co-teaching scenarios.

Scenario #2: "I Will Figure It Out"

Mr. Vetter and Ms. Guinta are meeting to discuss next week's plans. Mr. Vetter pushes a copy of his plans across the table and states, "It's pretty straightforward. I don't have anything to discuss unless you do."

Ms. Guinta reaches to grasp the plans.

She glances them over and says, "Well, Jason and Cynthia will need some additional examples, and they will all need additional time on Thursday when they take the test. I also have some concerns about Bryan—he just seems lost, and he hasn't been handing in his homework."

Mr. Vetter responded, "I knew about the homework, but other than that Bryan seems fine to me."

Mr. Vetter stands up, "I will ask Bryan about his homework today."

Ms. Guinta adds: "I just think he is not getting it during class—like maybe we need to add another strategy for him and others who could use additional practice."

Mr. Vetter, still standing, replies: "I will ask him about his homework, and you can let me know about the rest."

He began to walk toward the door.

"Yes," replied Ms. Guinta, "I will figure it out."

Mr. Vetter walked out of the room with 20 minutes left in their co-planning time. Ms. Guinta spent the remaining time working alone to consider strategies to guide the upcoming lessons.

Considerations for Questions for Discussion
1. Does Mr. Vetter's words match his actions? If so, how? If not, explain co-teacher's words
2. How did Mr. Vetter's actions inform Ms. Guinta's ways of communicating?

CDA Tools in Action: The Doing and Not Saying Tool

The Doing and Not Saying Tool can work to explain the relationship between the two teachers in this situation. Mr. Vetter comes prepared and provides a copy of his notes. He states the plans are straightforward and does not offer any willingness to go further with that discussion. At one point he stands up and a few minutes later begins to walk out of the room. He clearly does not want to discuss any instructional processes that may go along with his plans. In addition, he does not express any desire to further discuss Ms. Guinta's comments about exploring further instructional strategies to support students. The Doing and Not Saying Tool can empower Ms. Guinta to bring further awareness to Mr. Vetter's and her own actions. For example, it was clear to Ms. Guinta that Mr. Vetter did not want to discuss their plans in any detail. She allowed his actions to shape hers. Although she wanted to further discuss instructional strategies to align with the plans Mr. Vetter shared, she went along with his actions of standing up and then walking out of the room. With this new understanding, Ms. Guinta decided that she would follow up with Mr. Vetter to share specific strategies and to find out how they can support Bryan with his homework. Ms. Guinta became more aware of speaking up rather than being swayed by Mr. Vetter's actions toward limiting their conversations. With the support of the CDA tool, Ms. Guinta was inspired to directly address the "I will figure this out" to a "We will figure this out" approach. Before becoming aware of CDA tools to structure her actions, Ms. Guinta would continue to just go with the flow of her co-teacher's lack of interest in collaborating. Furthermore, through the lens of the CPZ, Ms. Guinta made use of the critical need for co-teachers to reconnect along a powerful collaborative process of connecting, disconnecting, and reconnecting. However, Mr. Vetter typically walked away from each opportunity to co-plan. Ms. Guinta began to follow up to stay connected and value each co-teacher's need to disconnect at times. Although Mr. Vetter was not completely on board, he did go along with Ms. Guinta's commitment to reconnecting, which provided additional connections for these co-teachers.

Scenario #3: "You Say, 'Why Fight It.' Then You Start Fading Away"

It was two months into the school year. Ms. Sallege found herself in a spin of frustration. "I just have this pit in my stomach every time I walk into the room," she shared in confidence with a friend outside of work.

> There is just no space for me to insert myself in any part of the lesson. I have so many ideas, and when I try to contribute, Ms. Peely either ignores me and keeps teaching or blatantly states that there is no time or just redirects the kids back to her. It's humiliating, really. I end up just walking around the room and helping students who need redirecting. Every day I think why fight it—but then I start fading away. You know how it is, you just can't help but feel insignificant.

After speaking with her friend, Ms. Sallege was determined to turn things around. Although eight weeks of school have passed and poor habits and routines have settled in, she decided there were many weeks ahead, and she had a lot to offer these students. The next day in school, she told Ms. Peely they needed to discuss how she would be taking on an active role in the classroom.

Discussion Questions:
1. How were Ms. Peely's actions shaping Ms. Sallege's actions?
2. How were Ms. Sallege's actions also shaping Ms. Peely's?
3. Were either co-teacher supporting the role of the other? Explain.
4. How did Ms. Sallege show signs of hoping to improve their co-teaching actions?

CDA Tool: The Context Is Reflexive Tool
Through the lens of the Context is Reflexive Tool, Ms. Sallege became aware that she was allowing the actions of Ms. Peely to shape her role as a passive participant in class. Furthermore, her actions shaped Ms. Peely's actions as lead and solo teacher in the class. Ms. Sallege began to write a list of ideas she had for ways she could insert strategies to guide students' learning. She shared two ideas and invited Ms. Peely to decide with her which strategy they should try first. Through this direct approach, Ms. Peely and Ms. Sallege began to expand the ways they worked together. Using this tool as a guide, Ms. Sallege facilitated more productive communication that led to improved co-teaching practices in their classroom over time.

Scenario #4: We're Like Two Pieces of a Puzzle

Ms. D. and Ms. K. shared a mutual respect for the role that each played in their teaching partnership. "We are both open to learning from one another," shared Ms. K. Ms. D elaborated by sharing how their co-planning connects with both teachers following through with their plans during instructional time (Stein, 2021, p. 81).

> We just talk about the ways we want to make lessons work for everybody. It just happens naturally because we just talk about it. Everyone sees us as a great team—everyone sees it. Parents are always saying we are like two pieces of a puzzle that fit perfectly together
> (p. 81)

Ms. K. continued to explain that she shares the plans for what they will be teaching by following their grade level curriculum and district expectations. Ms. D adds more about the process and how they could incorporate strategies that help the content be accessible to every learner in the room.

Questions for Discussion
1. How do Ms. K. and Ms. D. use their language and their actions to demonstrate what they find important to focus on?
2. How does each co-teacher work to connect with their teaching partner? How does their communication strengthen their co-teaching experience?
3. Does each co-teacher focus on relevant ideas and feelings in support of the role of their teaching partner?

CDA Tool: The Connection Building Tool
Ms. K. and Ms. D. naturally value the expertise of one another. They each enter their co-teaching relationship with an understanding about what they personally bring to their partnership. And each co-teacher is open to sharing and learning with one another. The connection building tool is naturally in place because each co-teacher feels relevant and valued with ongoing opportunities to contribute to the instructional process. They remain connected even when they each disconnect to plan for their part of daily lessons. For example, Ms. K plans the content and Ms. D then takes the plans and considers strategies that will empower learners to access the material. Ms. D and Ms. K come back together to share and implement their plans. The process of connecting, disconnecting, and reconnecting is at the core of succeeding within the CPZ Framework.

Let's consider the reality of two co-teachers who do not experience connecting as naturally as Ms. K. and Ms. D. The Connection Building Tool can guide the dialogic process when two teachers come together to discuss and bring awareness to the possible ways one or more of the co-teachers feel ignored or disconnected.

Key Takeaways

- Within the CPZ, power is a natural and encouraging part of the co-teaching partnership experience.
- The CPZ Framework embraces power as the process of each co-teacher leveraging their individual strengths and abilities in partnership with their co-teacher. This individual and blended approach optimizes the opportunity for co-teachers to experience a sustainable growth-fostering relationship that results in ongoing individual and collective growth.
- The tools within the communication zone and the CPZ serve as a strong structure and resource hub to empower and raise co-teaching awareness and actions to support thoughtful and sustainable partnerships.
- The CPZ provides the opportunities for co-powered experiences that start with a focus on reciprocity within the co-teaching relationship. This ongoing, cultivated relationship permeates through the instructional process and creation of the learning environment.
- The co-teacher power analysis tool optimizes co-teachers' awareness and understanding for how they are using and receiving their individual and collective power in ways that promote a natural process of ongoing improvement of co-teaching practices.
- Discourse analysis (also called discussion tools within the CPZ) optimizes co-teachers to communicate in ways that create spaces that become opportunities for co-teachers to experience respect through meaningful and thoughtful collaborations.
- Discussion tools shared in this chapter provide opportunities to practice an organic flow of each co-teacher "saying, doing, and being" to support collaborations while supporting ongoing growth of each co-teacher to feel grounded with a sense of being as the co-teaching relationship continues to be a growth-fostering experience with a sense of belonging and power with one another.

Co-teaching Connection Activity: Like it is! Your turn! What is your scenario?

Consider one recent scenario that you experienced. What happened between you and your co-teacher? Be specific, clear, and set yourself free in the text box below. Perhaps include information such as: What did you notice? What were your actions? What was your co-teacher doing? What were your interactions with one another? What were the students doing? How did you feel during this scenario and as a result of this experience?

Now, reread your scenario and decide which CDA tool could support your co-teaching conversation to transform your co-teaching practice. Which CDA tool would you use and why? Explain your thinking in the text box below.

Book Discussion Questions

1. Consider the definition of power within the CPZ. What strengths and skills are you currently applying within your co-teaching experience? What additional ways could you leverage your strengths?
2. How does acknowledging your sense of personal power help you to improve upon areas you would like to improve? How do you and your co-teacher support the personal and collective growth of one another through the acknowledgment of each individual's personal power?
3. Review the discourse analysis tool. Explain the difference between experiencing a "power to" and a "power with." What connections come to mind for you as you summarize this tool? What is a recent or upcoming scenario where this tool applies to your personal experiences?
4. Explain how the process of "saying, doing, and being" could empower each individual co-teacher. How can the process empower the partnership?
5. Review the discussion tools in this chapter. Which tool resonates with you the most? Why?
6. Which discussion tool seems to be the most challenging for you? How could you simplify the process to allow the empowering process to unfold between you and your co-teacher?

We Just Click! Co-teaching Characteristic Action: Empower: Earn your Empower jigsaw puzzle piece with a focus on how your communication practices serve to empower you as an individual and as a co-teaching team.

Activity: Expanding Your Comfort Zone

Look at Figure 9.4: Expanding your comfort zone. Consider how the communication tools described in Part 3, as well as the CPZ in general, may guide you and your co-teacher to have power with one another through dialogue. Think about how cogenerative dialogues, SiS approach, co-teaching discussion tools, and dialogic practices may serve to help each co-teacher experience their unique power as they negotiate and honor the power of one another. Remember, the aim is to allow ourselves to expand beyond feeling safe. Safety alone may often result in a status quo experience. The aim with the CPZ Framework is to guide co-teachers to experience a growth-fostering relationship. Also, remember that we must experience some degree of discomfort as we try to ways of teaching together. How can the tools in Part 3 help you to expand into the growth zone together? Discuss, and decide on your next action steps together. What tools shared in this book will help you?

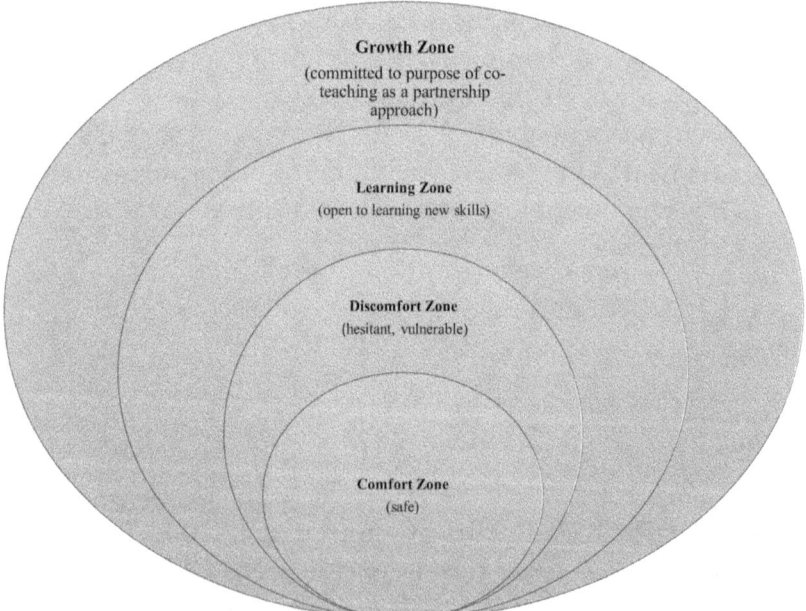

FIGURE 9.4 Expanding Your Comfort Zone.

10
Implementing Impactful Instructional Approaches for Co-teaching Power

The door opened slightly at first to allow one or two students through. Within seconds, it was pushed open all the way with the rush of running students ready to enjoy their recess break. As the fast-moving group raced from the building to the open field they screamed "We're free, We're free! We are finally free!"

There is no doubt that a break from learning in the classroom—or any kind of work—is a welcomed and needed pause and sense of freedom for anyone. The Co-teaching Power Zone (CPZ) embraces the notion that learning in the classroom can also provide a sense of liberation that naturally leads to meaningful engagement and joy that results from enriching dialogue and opportunities to be active participants in the learning process (Freire, 1970, 2007. This chapter reviews five evidence-based practices that optimize learners' freedom to think and meaningfully participate. All practices shared in this chapter are dialogic as they allow for ongoing open and active collaborations. They are also reflective and reflexive as the process organically invites learners to connect with their own thinking. Finally, they naturally unfold with learners actively participating as the result of sharing knowledge, making connections, and extending learning by listening to multiple perspectives.

The CPZ was created around the idea that the relationship between any two co-teachers permeates through their instructional decisions and their overall learning environment. This natural ebb and flow of connecting, disconnecting, and reconnecting optimizes the interactions and blended power between two co-teachers (Stein, 2021). This chapter reviews five instructional approaches that empower honoring two meaningfully active `teachers in a co-taught classroom while guiding them to experience growth-fostering relationships. This chapter will provide an overview of the approaches, and the next chapter will review scenarios for how they may be applied in any classroom through the lens of the CPZ The five instructional approaches are as follows:

1. Universal Design for Learning (Meyer et al., 2014)
2. Pedagogical Content Knowledge (Shulman, 1987)
3. Problem-posing instruction (Freire, 1970, 2011)
4. Cooperative learning (Johnson & Johnson, 1998)
5. Depths of knowledge (Hess, 2005)

Each of the instructional approaches provides opportunities for every learner in the room to be and feel valued as they connect with their personal perspective and expand their understanding by listening and learning from the perspectives of others in the class. The following approaches align with the CPZ because there are ongoing opportunities for learning to be transformed through the process of dialogue and time for all learners to naturally connect, disconnect, and reconnect with the learning process. Through these approaches, learners have the opportunity to be:

♦ **Free to explore**: Every learner has the opportunity to personally connect with the content. They have the opportunity to become motivated to learn by the flexibility provided within the structure of the lesson.
♦ **Empowered to express**: They are able to express their point of view and their understanding of the content being taught as the result of the liberating process of exploration and connection.

♦ **Energized by reflection**: Through the process of exploration and dialogue, learners monitor their evolving understandings.

These approaches guide teachers to naturally embed varying supports to guide each learner with opportunities for freedom of thinking at deeper, personalized levels. Furthermore, these approaches naturally embed the opportunities for each co-teacher to meaningfully contribute along every phase of the learning process.

Universal Design for Learning (UDL)

Neuroscience reveals that learners vary in the ways they engage with content, perceive information, and express their understanding of concepts being taught. When educators approach designing and implementing instruction with UDL, they naturally align the learning process with the three neural networks that guide every learner (Rose & Meyer, 2002; Meyer et al., 2014). When preparing lessons, teachers consider:

♦ **Engagement**: teachers vary the ways they go about motivating learners to actively participate and self-regulate their learning (affective network)
♦ **Representation**: teachers vary the way they present content area materials (recognition network)
♦ **Action & Expression**: teachers provide multiple ways for students to express their understanding of concepts and content.

The UDL guidelines (CAST, 2018) provide a visual display of the types of instructional decisions that may give boost to learners personally connecting with the learning process (see Figure 10.1).

UDL also optimizes instruction in a co-taught classroom because it empowers each co-teacher to contribute to the lesson in a variety of meaningful ways.

FIGURE 10.1 Universal Design for Learning Guidelines CAST (2018) www.cast.org.

1. **Know your students'** strengths, needs, and interests.
2. Consider the **context** of the lesson as you decide on how to teach the lesson.
3. Focus on **learning goal(s)** with an emphasis on the various ways learners may **process** the information as they all work toward the goals.
4. Be **flexible**, while maintaining the structure of your lesson, to allow learners to make sense of the information in personal ways.

Pedagogical Content Knowledge

Pedagogical Content Knowledge (PCK) (Shulman, 1987) illustrates how the subject of any given content area and lesson is transformed by the way the learners interact with the content. PCK is an experience with knowledge that is unique to teachers. It blends the teachers' knowledge of the subject matter of the lessons they teach with their knowledge of pedagogy. That is their understanding of the broad principles and strategies for effectively managing their classroom (Stein, 2017). According to Shulman, "effective teachers know their subjects and their students so well that they intentionally select the most useful forms of representation ... and make it comprehensible to others" (p. 9). Furthermore, teachers recognize the background knowledge that their students bring to specific lessons and what makes specific topics difficult for students to understand. Through the PCK lens, teachers are flexible with the knowledge of their subject matter, so they may guide the individual learners in their room to formulate their own ideas. Through a careful process of teaching and learning from the students, the teachers adjust their teaching to redirect individual students as the process unfolds.

PCK seamlessly aligns with the continuum of co-teaching and because it shares a dynamic movement of thinking, actions, and interactions, co-teachers may engage in with their students. PCK honors students' thinking by valuing their perspectives as they strive to teach the lesson in a manner that guides students to personally connect. Like UDL, PCK is deeply rooted in an assets-based approach, optimizing opportunities for every learner—including the two teachers—to feel comfortable to take risks and work through challenges within the process of learning.

How PCK Empowers Co-teachers

On a broad level, PCK includes seven knowledge layers. With seven opportunities to be knowledgeable, co-teachers may unite as a team by tapping into their personal strengths while supporting one another to strengthen other areas of knowledge. According to Shulman (1987), the seven knowledge layers are as follows:

1. **General pedagogical knowledge**: understanding of the broad principles and strategies for effectively managing learning and community in the classroom.
2. **Knowledge of learners**: Teachers know their students' abilities, interests, and areas in need of improvement.
3. **Knowledge of educational contexts**: Teachers know the structures and strategies that align with the context of specific lessons.
4. **Knowledge of outcomes, purpose, and values**: Teachers are clear about why they are teaching specific lessons, what students need to know as a result, and the importance of being a self-motivated learner.
5. **Content knowledge**: Teachers know the subject matter they teach
6. **Curriculum knowledge**: Teachers know the materials that align with subject matter and strategies for specific lessons.
7. **Pedagogical Content Knowledge**: Teachers know a variety of ways to represent information to guide learners to construct meaning. This PCK layer also aligns with empowering each co-teacher to connect with their personal strengths and qualities that they each bring to the learning process each day.

Using the knowledge layers, teachers strengthen their PCK by increasing their awareness and interpretations of how students' learning becomes transformed through their instructional decisions. PCK is deeply rooted in learners' experiences;

therefore, it becomes a very personalized process that optimizes the opportunity for learners to personally connect and become self-motivated. A PCK approach emphasizes that effective teachers cannot just know their content well—they must also have knowledge of how to teach the content to the specific students in their class. Cochran et al. (1993) expanded Shulman's original PCK approach to further connect with a constructivist approach. This revised lens further encourages teachers to blend a variety of knowledge layers in an evolving growth-oriented process. To create a deeper sense of teacher autonomy, they change the potentially static term "knowledge" to "knowing", therefore expanding to PCKg with the following definition: "A teacher's integrated understanding of four components of pedagogy, subject matter content, student characteristics, and the environmental context of learning" (p. 266). Teachers strengthen their effectiveness over time as they apply their understanding of the four components to their unique teaching experiences. This expanded version of PCK highlights the following key shifts in PCKg as:

1. **Dynamically action-oriented**: PCKg shifts from a possible static interpretation of teacher's knowledge to an ever evolving and ongoing learning process.
2. **Synthesizes**: PCKg streamlines the seven knowledge layers of the original model to four components of actionable knowledge, namely pedagogy, subject matter, students, and environmental contexts.
3. **Transformative**: Encourages all four components are integrated and, therefore, one component serves to strengthen the others in an ongoing learning process that guides teachers to continually improve their skills.

The CPZ integrates Shulman's original approach (1987) with a streamlined constructivist approach shared by Cochran et al. (1993). Furthermore, the CPZ integrates the tenets of UDL to further support co-teachers in designing and implementing effective instruction through the PCK approach. Specifically, we are all learners who come to the process with unique sets of strengths and areas to be improved upon. The context of the

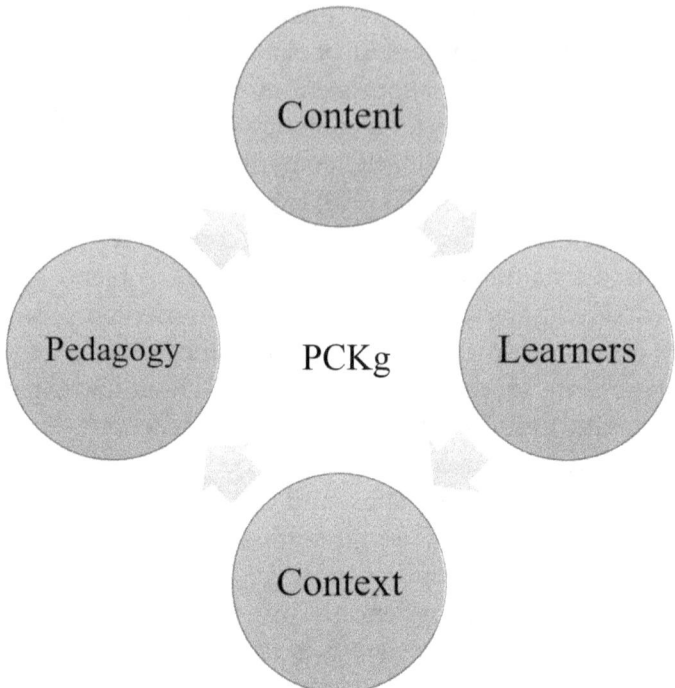

FIGURE 10.2 Four Components of Active Teaching

learning environment plays an integral part in illuminating the abilities of each learner as they further expand learning opportunities. See Figure 10.2.

The ongoing process of PCKg encourages teachers to be aware of all four actionable knowledge components simultaneously. Through this comprehensive focus, a teacher may transform learning within the interactions with all learners in the room. The CPZ includes PCKg as a structure that may empower all learners in the room—including the two teachers. It may become a powerful way for each co-teacher to contribute their personal expertise as they teach and learn alongside one another. Let's revisit the four PCKg components within the CPZ.

Applying PCK along the CPZ

The four components of PCKg may become an active part of guiding each co-teacher to actively contribute within all phases of daily instruction. Although each teacher is aware of experiencing all four components simultaneously, they may depend on each other to strengthen specific components as they experience working in partnership with their unique areas of expertise.

The Four Components along the CPZ
- **Knowing the Content**: Each teacher has knowledge for the subject area they teach. If one co-teacher experiences gaps in subject area knowledge, they actively seek the resources and remain a learner along the process.
- **Knowing the Learners**: Each teacher knows the interests, strengths, and area in need of improvement of their co-teaching partner. Furthermore, each teacher knows the individual students in their room. This knowledge optimizes teachers' communication and interactions as well as their intentional instructional decisions based on the individuals in their class.
- **Knowing the Context**: Each teacher actively seeks to optimize the materials, strategies, and physical arrangements in the room to meet the specific strengths and needs of their students. They intentionally implement additional visual, auditory, or kinesthetic supports based on their knowledge of their students and the ways that would optimize students to transform the representation of material into personal and meaningful information.
- **Knowing Pedagogy**: Each teacher has a broad understanding of evidence-based, effective methods for teaching. They are aware of their personal style for delivering curriculum, guiding students' learning, communicating with their students, and guiding their students to reach their full potential. Along the CPZ, this component also includes being aware of our co-teacher's pedagogical beliefs. The CPZ guides the two teachers to honor, validate, and blend their pedagogical actions as they work together as a team.

Through the PCKg lens, each teacher is aware of each component simultaneously and over time strengthens their ability to naturally embed their skills of all four components as one layered flow of effective teaching. The CPZ brings further possibilities of the possibilities for effectively teaching by combining the two unique PCKg layers of each co-teacher. The CPZ process optimizes the ability for each teacher to enter the PCK process at any entry point. It honors the individual strengths of each co-teacher as it guides and empowers their growth-fostering relationship. For example, the general educator may begin at content knowledge and the special educator may enter the PCK approach with knowledge of learners and they both share their knowledge and move along in collaboration from there. Let's take a look into observable classroom behaviors with co-teachers and their students as the PCKg is naturally embedded.

Observable Classroom Student Behaviors

When aligning with the PCKg approach, there are six observable classroom behaviors for co-teachers to consider whether their selected instructional practices are most effective for their specific groups of students. The first step is for co-teachers to ask: *What is it we want to teach? What is the skill and content students need to know?* The next critical step is to ask: *How will we know when we have taught it?* The following six student behaviors will guide co-teachers to evaluate their teaching behaviors and implementation of the four PCKg components together in partnership.

Students' observable learning	Examples of teachers' instructional actions
Comprehension of content	• Preview and Review material • Present clear, visible goals • Encourage students to paraphrase learning goals • Activate and assess students' background knowledge
Transformation of Learning	• Provide additional examples • Allow time for students to provide examples • Encourage students to make connections, share examples of application in other settings, add on to their previous understanding to demonstrate deeper learning
Instructional Process	• Students are actively engaged in individual, partners, small group, and whole class learning. There is an active participation component to all learning

Evaluation	• Provide opportunities for students to paraphrase and express how they feel their learning is going • Apply formative assessments
Reflection	• Students have the opportunity to review, consider other ways of thinking to expand their perspective • Students share how their learning applies to future learning • Students share the skills they notice they are strengthening as a result of actively participating • Students express a goal for future learning based on their curiosity or questions
New Comprehension	• As a result of the reflection process, students identify new facts, questions, concepts they learned as a result of participating in the learning.

Problem-Posing Instruction

Problem-posing education is a process that encourages learners to feel a sense of freedom to think and act within a meaningful learning process. According to Freire (1970, 2011), a traditional banking educational process where teachers pass along information to students for them to learn and memorize inhibits the process of meaningful learning. During the process of a banking model, Freire explains students are passive learners as a result of the teacher teaching and the students merely receiving information rather than interacting with ideas. The banking model keeps the teacher as the one who knows the content and assumes the students do not hold knowledge—therefore, they must be compliant as knowledge is deposited into their minds by the teacher. In the banking model, knowledge is transferred from the teacher to the students. Yet, students often receive the transfer in often robotic ways. Freire shares a problem-posing process as the solution to the banking model. The solution involves teachers who learn from and with their students. This reciprocal approach allows the teacher to still teach; however, allow for exploration and discovery to be a part of the learning. Through this discovery time, students experience deeper cognitive thought processing. They have the opportunity to become meaningfully engaged rather than compliant, passive listeners.

Problem-posing instruction emphasizes reciprocity, where students and teachers learn from and with each other as they share ideas and express their understanding (p. 73). Six key characteristics of problem-posing education includes:

- Learners are capable
- Learning occurs through problem-solving
- Learning relates to practical, real-life applications
- Students and teachers are co-learners
- Reciprocity exists where the teacher learns from the students and the students learn from the teacher.
- Learning is a process of becoming. It is acknowledged that every individual is a part of an ongoing ability to keep on learning.

Another key idea of problem-posing instruction emphasizes that a teacher cannot think for their students. Teachers share knowledge, and then they must acknowledge that students need time to personally make sense of what was just taught. Teachers cannot simply impose their thinking on their students. Teachers value their students as individual thinkers. It is through dialogue and communication where a shared responsibility to teach and learn occurs. In this manner, learning is transformed through shared ideas and expanded perspectives.

Cooperative Learning

Cooperative learning is a structure that employs the power of working in groups to strengthen students' learning at the individual and group levels. Within cooperative group learning, individuals work toward shared goals with their group members. Cooperation during small group learning results in an opportunity for learners to put forth greater effort, be more productive in learning the academic content, cultivate peer relationships, and have increased intrinsic motivation, confidence, and social skills such as effective communication (Johnson & Johnson, 1998).

Teachers have the flexibility to form three types of cooperative learning groups.

1. **Formal**: The heart of cooperative learning rests in forming formal groups. These groups may form for one class period or lesson, or they may bond over several weeks. Learners within formal groups work ensure each learner is actively involved in the academic learning and increase critical thinking skills as each student organizes materials, summarize, explain, and synthesize information.
2. **Informal**: These groups form as necessary and may meet for a few minutes to a full class or lesson. Learners engage in previewing or reviewing academic content. Informal groups work when the teacher spontaneously or intentional plans for brief times that allow students to discuss to process to guide them to make sense of content taught directly by the teachers.
3. **Base**: These long-term groups last for the duration of the class for the year or marking period. These groups allow learners to feel connected with a strong sense of belonging within this peer support membership. Teachers may have students sit within their base groups to start the class time and then add time for base groups to shift into formal or informal groups depending on the context of the lesson. Cooperative learning groups further optimize co-teachers' ability to contribute their unique teaching and learning skills. Each co-teacher may easily be meaningfully active participants as they work to increase learning for every learner in the room.

Optimizing Student Interactions

Simply placing students in groups does not mean learning will take place. Each student is encouraged to be an active learner who has the opportunity to contribute to their own learning and the learning of their peers. According to Johnson and Johnson (1998), a learning experience can only qualify as cooperative to the extent that five elements exist.

Five Elements of Cooperative Learning

1. **Positive interdependence**: Each member understands that their group mates count on their contributions to accomplish the task. Every member's contribution is needed to achieve group goal(s).
2. **Individual accountability**: Each member experiences a sense of responsibility for their own learning as they work toward achieving shared goal(s). In addition, each member is responsible for learning the material shared by their group members.
3. **Promotive interaction**: Asynchronous work will likely be a part of the learning process where each member works individually. However, there must be a percentage of time where the group meets in person (or at least synchronously via digital tools) for them to share and provide feedback to one another. These interactions need to result in dialogue that includes individuals questioning, reasoning, and drawing conclusions on the group's key understandings.
4. **Collaborative skills**: Students are guided to develop collaborative skills with opportunities to build trust, exercise leadership, express decision-making, and communicate effectively by honoring one another's perspectives and develop conflict-management skills.
5. **Group processing**: Students are guided to assess their performance. They review what is going well and what may need to change to make their performance even better.

Cooperative learning groups maximize learning as the result of the effective structure of guiding students' actions and interactions. A fifth instructional approach that empowers co-teachers through the lens of CPZ is the use of questioning—specifically Bloom's Taxonomy and depths of knowledge (DOK) to activate deeper thinking and learning through dialogue.

Bloom's Taxonomy and Depths of Knowledge (DOK)

Based on the levels of Bloom's Taxonomy (Anderson & Krathwohl, 2001) there are six types of thinking that occur during the learning process. These levels are placed along a hierarchy to acknowledge knowledge as the first and most simple type of thinking. An individual may move up the levels through comprehension, application, analysis, synthesis, and final type of thinking, evaluation as the most complex. Bloom's Taxonomy served to illuminate the value of becoming more aware of the type of thinking needed to deepen a learning process (Stein, 2017). Anderson and Krathwohl (2002) revised the taxonomy to further explain how learners actively interact with the content they are learning as well as engage in active thinking and speaking when in dialogue. The updated Bloom's Taxonomy includes changing the levels of thinking from nouns to verbs—indicating a learner's actions and interactions with their thinking, the content, and in dialogue with others. Another change is the order of the final two types of thinking. The six types of thinking now flow from the simplest task to remember through the levels, understand, apply, analyze, evaluate, and create (see Figure 10.3). The idea is that learners are active along deeper levels of thinking and interacting within the learning process. As the hierarchy illustrates, it is understood that the levels of thinking build upon one another. A learner must become skilled at the lower levels before moving up to the next levels toward the most complex type of thinking.

The use of Bloom's Taxonomy has been effective in guiding teachers to vary the types of questions they pose to students

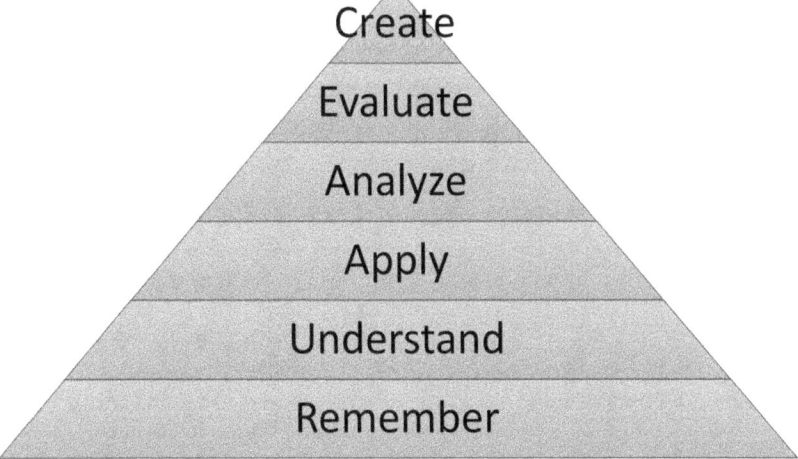

FIGURE 10.3 Six Types of Thinking along Bloom's Taxonomy

during instruction. Teachers become more mindful to increase their own thinking as they guide their students to develop critical thinking skills (Stein, 2017; Song, 2019; Bibi et al., 2020). The structure of Bloom's Taxonomy guides educators to be aware of the cognitive level they are encouraged by their students. Depths of Knowledge (DOK) is another framework for encouraging critical thinking and active learning. DOK takes the levels of thinking in Bloom's Taxonomy and places them into four DOK levels. Each level is considered important without the feeling of moving through lower steps to get to higher levels. In contrast with Bloom's Taxonomy that measures a learner's cognitive level (type of thinking), Webb (1997) developed the DOK framework to illustrate the context of learning as a guide for situating the interactions students will engage to express their understanding. The process of learning within the DoK framework does not have that linear feel that may exist when learning through a hierarchical framework. There are four levels that may guide educators to vary the ways they are asking their students to think and interact. The following table outlines the four levels.

Hess (2006) encourages process-oriented thinking by describing each level not as a step but as a "ceiling" that establishes how in-depth students will interact with the content and the context in which they will be sharing their thinking. The instructional approaches shared in this chapter optimize the opportunity for two teachers to work together in dialogue with one another and with their students. The instructional approaches work to support any content area lesson where two teachers are striving to allow their relationship to strengthen and transform their co-teaching practices.

Level 1: Gathering information	Students are recalling, gathering, and reproducing information and text evidence. This is a literal and factual level of thinking.
Level 2: Using information	Students are explaining ideas and beginning to share how to apply information.

Level 3: Being strategic with information	Students are thinking more critically by explaining how to use information. They are beginning to critique various perspectives and expand their own perspective in the process.
Level 4: Extending strategic and creative ways to use information	Students apply knowledge across content areas, time, and settings. They create new ways of thinking about previous learned ideas. They explore their knowledge in relation to their ongoing experiences of gathering and making sense of information.

Key Takeaways

- As mentioned throughout previous chapters, within the CPZ, the co-teaching relationship permeates through instruction and overall learning environment.
- The process of collaboration includes the natural process of individuals connecting, disconnecting, and reconnecting to optimize interactions within the group and the blended power of the two co-teachers.
- This chapter reviews five instructional approaches that empower and honor two meaningfully active co-teachers along a process of creating a safe and supportive learning environment with their students.
- The five instructional approaches discussed in this chapter include UDL, PCK, problem-posing instruction, cooperative learning, and Blooms Revised Taxonomy and DOK. Each instructional approach provides a structure to optimize space and time for every learner to personally make sense of the content along a dialogic process.
- The five instructional approaches discussed in this chapter expand every learner's ability to feel a sense of belonging as an active learner with the opportunities to feel free to explore content and their thoughts around the content, freedom to express their understanding, and time to reflect on what they learned as they connect with their personal abilities and build upon their background knowledge and skills for future learning opportunities.

Co-teaching Connection Activity: Living Your Best Co-teaching Life!

As you consider the ways you and your co-teacher may join together to be two active, autonomous teaching partners, select one of the dialogic practices described in this chapter and share how you and your co-teacher may apply in an upcoming lesson. Use the following chart to formatively assess your and your co-teacher's performance.

Yes	*Neutral*	*No*
Oh, yeah! We were both meaningfully active and authentically and actively engaged our students in the learning process as well.	Well, I'm not sure. We need to try the instructional practice at least two more times before we see if it is effective.	One of us was much more involved than the other. The students were not as engaged as they could have been.

Your Selected Instructional Practice_____
(see the ideas from this chapter)

Book Discussion Questions

1. Within the CPZ, co-teachers have the opportunity to engage in a growth-fostering relationship where they first and foremost belong to one another. This relationship then permeates through the instructional process and overall learning environment. Describe how you are personally experiencing your co-teaching relationship. How does it affect the instructional process in your class? Describe with evidence of your actions, your co-teacher's actions, your interactions, and the actions of your students.
2. The process of connecting, disconnecting, and reconnecting is a unique and empowering collaborative process for co-teaching success. Describe a recent experience where you and your co-teacher effectively experienced this collaborative process in preparation for a lesson. How did you both feel as you reconnected to share what you did or learned during the time you disconnected? How did this affect your instructional time?
3. Review the five instructional approaches shared in this chapter. In your opinion, how do they create space and time for co-teachers and all learners to engage in the collaborative process of connecting, disconnecting, and reconnecting?
4. When considering instructional approaches within the CPZ, explain the importance of ensuring a dialogic process. How does this process create a sense of freedom for co-teachers and all learners to connect with themselves as learners?

11

Applying Evidence-Based Practices within the Co-teaching Power Zone

This chapter brings all other chapters together by sharing authentic—real teachers—real perspectives—real applications for how co-teachers may utilize the structure of the communication zone and the Co-teaching Power Zone (CPZ) framework to empower their individual and collective co-teaching actions. After reading through all scenarios in this chapter, you will have an opportunity to experience "ah-ha" moments in how the communication zone and the five impactful instructional strategies allow the co-teachers to strengthen their co-teaching through the CPZ. Following each scenario and/or at the end of the chapter, consider the following guiding questions to guide your deeper understanding and readiness to apply the CPZ with your co-teacher(s).

Four Guiding Questions

1. How can the co-teaching models be seamlessly and organically aligned within the CPZ?
2. How do the five impactful instructional strategies (PCK, UDL, Bloom's Taxonomy and DOK, cooperative learning,

DOI: 10.4324/9781003333692-15

and problem posing instruction—see Chapter 9) empower autonomy for all learners—including the two co-teachers along the CPZ?
3. How does the communication zone and the CPZ organically address the power dynamics between co-teachers?
4. How does the power of connecting, disconnecting, and reconnecting further empower co-teaching collaborations and learning with students in any co-taught classroom?

Since the collaboration zone and CPZ is a process—let's begin with a few scenarios to guide you to put it all together as you consider how you will utilize. Following each scenario, I will share the specific ways the collaboration zone and CPZ were applied. There will also be an opportunity for you to consider your thoughts as you begin thinking about your own applications.

Example #1: Third Time's the Charm

It was not Ms. Kotare's imagination. Every time she stepped into class just before the bell rang, Ms. Levine made the same face—as if she just had a spoonful of something that was way too spicy. Ms. Kotare vowed to herself that she would not take it personally, but the pattern over time was unmistakable. She decided to approach Ms. Levine after class.

During the brief two minutes they had, Ms. Levine validated Ms. Kotare's observation by stating, "No, you're right." She chuckled nervously and added, "When I see you coming into the room, I honestly twitch." It's just I know you have ideas for how to teach these kids, and I just get nervous because there is so much to teach and doing things differently will likely take up some of the precious time we have."

Ms. Kotare thanked Ms. Levine for sharing and added. "Okay, I hear that. But what good is teaching the content if most students are not connecting with the lesson anyway?" I also have a hard time doing my part in ensuring that students are accessing the learning during class time. How about if we keep your lessons as they are—because they are great as is—but add strategies to encourage students to process and connect with the content? Students would still get the same necessary content, but they will be actively processing it at strategic points in the lesson that we decide—rather than passively sitting and disconnected to learning."

"I don't know. Now you are making me twitch even more," Ms. Levine replied.

Ms. Kotare explained, "No pressure to start this week. By tomorrow, I will share one simple strategy that will keep any lesson you plan intact, and it will open up possibilities for students to really connect."

"Okay," Ms. Levine reluctantly responded.

"Well, how about we try the strategy three times before you decide if you like it. Because after the first time, you will probably still be twitching. After the second time, you may start to be a bit more comfortable. After the third time, you will have a broader understanding after applying three times. So, we will try the first-time next week. Then, we will plan for two more occasions before we discuss whether to keep implementing the strategy."

"Okay. Next week we are in our poetry unit, so I will send you the poems and the focus for each lesson," Ms. Levine replied as she began to greet the next group of students coming into class for 7th period.

"Great. I have to run to my next class, but I will email you later on today with a basic strategy for us to start with," Ms. Kotare replied with a smile as she ran from the room.

Over the next few days, the two teachers collaborated asynchronously by sharing the lesson content and strategies. Ms. Kotare decided to start small and embed a basic turn and talk strategy. She chose this strategy because it required no prep and would be the least invasive to Ms. Levine's lesson. They both agreed to launch the co-teaching approach on Monday.

The lesson began, as usual with Ms. Levine introducing the focus for the day's lesson. The one difference that Ms. Kotare noticed was that Ms. Levine frequently made eye contact as if to say: *Jump in when you want to*. Ms. Levine taught as usual. She presented the day's text and reviewed information about the author of the text. "Today we will read a poem by Edgar Allen Poe," Ms. Levine explained. "Poe is known for his talent with symbolism in his writing."

After reviewing more information about the poet, Ms. Levine said, "Okay, we are ready to begin reading." As Ms. Levine presented a visual slide of the text, Ms. Kotare walked around to provide the students with individual copies. Ms. Levine asked, "Ms. Kotare, are we ready to begin?"

Ms. Kotare replied, "How about we slide our desks closer to the peer in the next row?"

"Great idea," replied Ms. Levine. She then guided rows of students to slide together, so each student was paired with one peer.

Ms. Kotare added, "Okay, as Ms. Levine reads each stanza of the poem, your job is to just listen and underline, circle, or annotate in the margins any thoughts that come to mind from reading and listening." Ms. Kotare drew a line after the first stanza. Ms. Levine directed the students to do the same. Ms. Levine began to read as Ms. Kotare modeled the listening process on the board. She underlined words, starred specific lines in the stanza, and wrote notes in the margin next to the first stanza. At the end of the first stanza, Ms. Levine continued to move along to the second stanza.

After the second stanza, Ms. Kotare stated, "How about we give each pair time to share their thinking so far." Ms. Kotare continued to direct the class, "Okay, so each pair needs to decide who will be partner A and who will be partner B." After 30 seconds, Ms. Kotare stated, "Okay partner As raise your hand." Hands went up around the room. "Partner Bs raise your hands." Once everyone was ready, Ms. Levine and Ms. Kotare made eye contact with a nod. Ms. Levine added, "Okay, get ready to discuss." Ms. Kotare added, "Partner A share your thoughts first while Partner B listens. Then switch and Partner B shares while Partner A listens." The shuffling of students sitting up in their seats was visible and audible. The two co-teachers once again nodded toward each other, and Ms. Levine said, "Okay! Discuss!" Both co-teachers walked around the room as the students took turns sharing their annotations and other markings from reading the first two stanzas.

After 30 seconds, Ms. Kotare shared, "Okay, if you didn't already do so, Partner B, it's your turn to share and Partner A's turn to listen." As the next 30 seconds ended, the two co-teachers nodded to each other. Ms. Levine directed the class, "Okay, let's read the next two stanzas."

Ms. Kotare added, "Get ready to mark up your page with your thinking again." The students were attentive, and ready to read and listen with pen in hand. The process continued in that manner with strategic stops for peers to collaborate after reading every two stanzas. Finally, with 3 minutes before the bell was going to ring, Ms. Kotare said, "Okay, let's sum up in one word how you feel about today's class. On the count of 3, please share your word with your partner. One … two … three!" The buzz of sharing was evident. Ms. Kotare asked students to then take out a sticky note and write their name on it. She asked them to jot down one thing they learned from listening to their partner's ideas about the poem today—and then hand it in as they walked out the door.

After the first day, Ms. Levine told Ms. Kotare, "I know the kids were more engaged, but we didn't get as far in the reading. But I do see how giving students time to talk together doesn't take away as much time as I thought it would. I'm still twitching, but I am ready to try this again next time."

After the third time, Ms. Levine admitted, "I actually want to do this with my other classes. I am just nervous to do it without you."

Evidence of Impactful Instruction along the CPZ
Reciprocity
- The application of the co-teaching model, team teaching, allowed for both co-teachers to volley back and forth while guiding the class together.
- Students were provided the space to value their thinking along with a peer's thoughts and connect with the whole class reading process.
- Each co-teacher's teaching style was valued and applied. Specifically, Mrs. Levine's tendency toward a teacher-

centered process with Ms. Kotare's student-centered approach.
- Ongoing communication and checking in after each lesson.
- The flow of collaboration—specifically, connecting to co-plan, then disconnecting to each plan their part in the lesson, and reconnecting to co-teach and then debrief and reflect on their work together to plan ahead for future lessons. Each teacher was meaningfully active with effective contributions and opportunities to expand their own teaching and learning.
- As a result of the teachers' reciprocity and clear communication, the students were brought in to this reciprocal flow in effective ways.
- Reciprocity continues to empower and permeate through the instructional process and co-creation of the learning environment.

Impact on Instruction
- **PCK** naturally empowers each co-teacher to contribute their knowledge and expertise. Specifically, Ms. Levine shared her knowledge of the content while Ms. Kotare added her knowledge of the content with an emphasis on her knowledge of pedagogy and teaching strategies that guide every learner to connect with the materials and deepen their learning. Furthermore, Ms. Kotare's knowledge of the context of learning specifically the co-teaching model that aligned with this lesson and the turn and talk strategy expanded Ms. Levine's knowledge of context as well as evidenced through their nonverbal, ongoing, reciprocal communication with each other and the way they interacted with the students.

Evidence of Students' observable learning through the lens of PCK

1. Students paraphrased their understanding of the poem as they worked with a partner.

2. Transformation of learning occurred as students made connections, shared their thinking, and considered one thing they learned from their partner in discussion.
3. Students were actively annotating, reading, listening, and speaking throughout the lesson.
4. Students evaluated their learning through the "one word" brief strategy at the end. In addition, students shared how their partner's thinking extended their learning.

- **Cooperative learning** techniques were applied through the use of the turn and talk peer collaboration process. Each student was assigned to be either Partner A or Partner B. The way Ms. Kotare facilitated the process held each student accountable to participate as listener and speaker.
- **UDL** was applied by Ms. Kotare adding additional ways for the students to perceive, engage, and express their understanding. Let's take a look through the lens of the three UDL principles.

Multiple Means of Engagement

1. The turn and talk process optimized value, relevance, and authenticity in the way students connected with the learning.
2. The ebb and flow of teacher directed and student directed discussion processes minimized threats and distractions by valuing every thinker in the room.

Multiple Means of Representation

1. Ms. Levine prepared visual slides to display the poem. Ms. Kotare added individual copies for each student to visually follow as well as mark up and annotate.
2. Ms. Kotare modeled annotating and marking up the poem on the board.

Multiple Means of Action & Expression

1. Students were guided to manage new information as Ms. Kotare modeled annotating and marking up the poem.
2. Students monitored their understanding through peer collaborations

Impact on the Learning Environment

This scenario shares the ways Ms. Kotare applied her personal power as a special educator to work alongside her co-teacher. She applied language like "How about we try this…" with the intention of easing into some meaningful additions to the instructional repertoire already in place. In addition, Ms. Kotare pushed through the discomfort of guiding a co-teacher to expand ways of teaching and learning with the focus on guiding all learners in the room to connect with the content. Ms. Levine, although uncomfortable at first, was willing to negotiate the power of teaching by relinquishing some instructional decisions to her co-teacher. The classroom environment flowed with the two teachers modeling meaningful communication and shared collaboration. This working relationship permeated through the learning environment by its natural co-creation of a risk-free learning environment where all thinking is valued. This was evidenced as students were provided time to organize their own thinking and share with a partner. Furthermore, students were asked to provide feedback at the end of the lesson to evaluate and self-monitor their learning. Students engaged in the collaboration process that is central to the CPZ. Specifically, the students engaged in a flow of connecting individually to gain personal insights. During this individual connection, students optimized time to disconnect with others to consider their personal ideas and then to reconnect with their partner during the turn and talk discussion to share and to expand their understanding by listening to their partner's ideas.

Example #2: "This Is the Way I've Always Taught, and It Has Always Worked"

Ms. Kuhn was not used to co-teaching. In fact, the last time she co-taught she remembers "It didn't really work. I just love social studies and teaching it—I have just never found anyone who I can share that with—I would rather just teach by myself—it works better that way." This year, Ms. Kuhn was paired with a new special educator in the district. Ms. Robbins was looking forward to co-teaching social studies and English classes this year. She grew up learning about historical events during many family dinners. Ms. Robbins was excited to share her passion for social studies with the class. Furthermore, she and Mr. Adler were co-teaching with ease in her English class. They co-planned and implemented lessons with a strong balance of structure and flexibility. There were many opportunities for the students to engage in learning through the many instructional strategies Ms. Robbins brought into each lesson. She and Mr. Adler implemented varied co-teaching models such as parallel teaching to teach the same lesson, but within a smaller group and with the flexibility for each teacher to engage the students with specific strategies that worked for each group. Mr. Adler and Ms. Robbins also effectively implemented team teaching to ensure that every student had the opportunity to process the information through varied examples, and additional strategies to guide students to think deeply about the content. For example, during a recent lesson where the students needed to compare and contrast two texts, Mrs. Robbins and Mr. Adler worked together to each come up with leveled questions to guide students' thinking around each text. Students worked individually and in groups to discuss their responses. "Curiosity is in the air every time I walk into the room," Ms. Robbins stated. "I just love guiding students to think and to share their thinking with others in their group."

Ms. Robbins was so confused why she and Ms. Kuhn were not getting along. "I come into the room, and she basically ignores me. She sends me her plans for the week, but she doesn't want to discuss *how* we will teach. She just wants me to go back to my previous district, I think." The worst part is when I am in that social studies class, I feel like an uninvited guest. I make sure I wear quiet shoes because I feel like I can't draw any attention to myself as I just walk around the room feeling invisible. It is just heartbreaking to see the kids just zoning out at their seats. It is always the same five kids who raise their hands and get to speak." When Ms. Robbins approaches Ms. Kuhn with possible ways they could teach together, Ms. Kuhn replies, "I don't think that is necessary. This is the way I have always taught, and it has always worked."

Ms. Robbins decides to take a more direct approach, while still respecting Ms. Kuhn's perspective. Afterall, she cannot force Ms. Kuhn; yet at the same time, she must advocate for her role as a co-teacher as well. Ms. Robbins is determined to support students' learning, so she calls for a team meeting, so that she can meet with all of her co-teachers at the same time. At this meeting, they will discuss how they are experiencing co-teaching. Ms. Kuhn reluctantly attends the meeting, but agrees to meet with Ms. Robbins again to discuss how they may co-teach actively together for an upcoming lesson.

Reciprocity

Mr. Adler and Ms. Robbins share the gift of reciprocity. It comes naturally for these two to engage in the natural flow of connecting, disconnecting, and reconnecting through their co-planning and implementing interactions. They value each other's contributions with potential for improving their teaching and learning in the classroom.

Ms. Kuhn, on the other hand, is not open to sharing any part of the teaching responsibilities with Ms. Robbins. Ms. Kuhn's tenacity leads to a team meeting, which then opens the door to possibilities between these two co-teachers. Although it will not necessarily be an easy process, Ms. Robbins respects Ms. Kuhn's perspective, while also respecting her role through a process of open, transparent communication to broaden the ways they teach together.

Impact on Instructional Practices

The relationship shared between Mr. Adler and Ms. Robbins unfolds in a variety of effective ways. They vary their co-teaching models and intentionally select models that match specific lessons. For example, the use of parallel teaching was applied to teach the same lesson, while meeting the specific needs of the students in smaller groups. Each teacher was able to select instructional strategies that served to support the process of learning—while still achieving the same learning objective. They applied leveled questioning through Blooms Revised Taxonomy to meet each student at the level of thinking they were at—while supporting them to think more deeply by listening to others.

According to this scenario, Ms. Robbins and Ms. Kuhn experienced very limited co-teaching practices. One teach and one circulate was the one co-teaching default model. Ms. Robbins was not a part of the instructional process—other than the potential for her to walk around and notice how students were engaging and performing with the lesson. Given what we now know about the CPZ, we can consider the many options for systematically supporting these two teachers. Ms. Robbins began to take these steps as she created a team meeting to serve as a launching point for more personal and ongoing communication with Ms. Kuhn.

Impact on the Learning Environment

It isn't difficult to see that the relationship between Mr. Adler and Ms. Robbins resulted in a free flowing, yet structured collaborative process of learning. Students worked together in dialogue as they became a part of the process the two teachers created. On the other hand, Ms. Robbins and Ms. Kuhn created a different feel in the classroom. It was tense and filled with passive learners—including Ms. Robbins.

It is interesting to see how the same co-teacher—with the same enthusiasm and dedication to teaching and learning—can experience co-teaching in vastly different ways within the same day. The CPZ can be used to support the process as co-teachers navigate, empower, and improve the unique co-teaching experiences.

Example #3: It's Not Jake Who Is Struggling—It's Our Lesson Design!

This is the second year of co-teaching together. Mr. Lupome and Ms. Bachman began the year in the same manner as they ended the last year. The co-teachers alternated roles. As one teacher taught aspects of the lesson, the other teacher walked around supporting students at their seats. The two co-teachers worked well together. Each is open to working together to teach and support students. After two weeks of the school year, Ms. Bachman said, "Do you notice how Jake is struggling? He just copies from the board, and when I work side by side with him during the lesson, he says he understands, yet his work does not demonstrate that."

"Funny you should mention that," said Mr. Lupome. "I did notice Jake and a few others who just wait for us to explain something or write on the board. They are not doing the thinking—we are."

"Maybe they should come for extra help. I don't know what else we can do," said Ms. Bachman.

"Actually, the way I see it," said Mr. Lupome, "it is not Jake who is struggling—it's our lesson design!" He sat down beside Ms. Bachman and began to explain.

"Think about it. We are modeling what they need to do—and the same students respond to questions we ask—and the rest of them either work independently because they are sparked and know what to do—or they are confused and need more time to think about how to apply the math."

"That makes sense," replied Ms. Bachman. "But we just do not have time to slow down, and that wouldn't even be fair to the rest of the class."

"There is another way," explained Mr. Lupome. "How about we put the students into groups. And instead of calling on one student at a time during our whole class teaching, we pause to allow students to discuss in groups? Then you and I may walk around listening in and supporting students as needed."

The next day the two teachers applied Mr. Lupome's idea and noticed not only were all students engaging in dialogue about solving the math problems, but the teachers were able to learn which students had a clear understanding of the concept and which students needed further clarification. The teachers enjoyed the freedom of walking around and supporting students in the moments of teaching.

Reciprocity

Mr. Lupome demonstrated reciprocity in the ways they applied their team-teaching practices. They created a history of valuing the contributions of each teacher during the teaching process. Furthermore, they shared a process of open communication as Ms. Bachman remained flexible in listening to Mr. Lupome's ideas for another way to make the math content accessible to all students. Ms. Bachman responded with a willingness to look beyond her traditional view of Jake as a struggling learner to see that perhaps it was the lesson design that created the struggle. With the co-teachers' interactions, the students were brought into the process of reciprocity by the opportunity to be thinkers and active learners along the process.

Impact on Instructional Practices

The teachers implemented team teaching and station teaching with intention and teamwork. They strategically planned the role of each teacher, while both remained active along the teaching and learning process.

UDL was embedded as the co-teachers considered other ways of engaging the learners. They moved from the whole class to small groups. This optimized student attention and motivation as well as including peer collaborations. The teachers further embedded student engagement by walking around to provide mastery-oriented feedback to the students.

PCK was evident by the way Mr. Lupome contributed his knowledge of students, content, and context in order to maximize accessibility and learning. Learning the content was a clear focus; yet the way the teachers honored *how* the students learned it was a critical aspect of making learning accessible for all students.

Problem Posing Instruction occurred as the teachers gave the students mathematical problems to solve in groups. No longer were students expected to copy from the board and wait for other students to answer, but every student was not involved in actively thinking through toward solutions and content mastery.

Impact on Learning Environment
Mr. Lupome and Ms. Bachman moved with ease to plan and implement structures and strategies that aligned with the context of their lessons and their students. They fostered collaboration between themselves which permeated through to the opportunity for all learners in the class to feel a sense of community.

Using the Five Impactful Instructional Strategies for along the CPZ
Each school day moves at a very quick pace. Educators in general must strategically manage their countless responsibilities and decisions each day. Multiply that times two in a co-taught classroom and we can either experience twice the strain or double the support. The five impactful instructional strategies are examples that provide co-teachers ways to work together with one another to strengthen their relationship during class time. These instructional approaches optimize effective and meaningful co-teaching practices by naturally including students' active thinking and participation to empower the learning process.

Key Takeaways

- ♦ The motivation, collaboration, and communication zones within the CPZ are a process and experienced differently depending on the unique co-teacher's individual and collective power.
- ♦ The co-teaching relationship will always yield evidence for how it permeates through the instruction and overall learning environment. Stay aware and willing to accept and improve the ways each co-teacher may be and inspire one another's abilities along the teaching and learning process.
- ♦ The scenarios shared in this chapter share unique, authentic experiences of co-teachers within the CPZ.

Co-teaching Connection Activity: Co-teaching Promise Starters

Using the co-teaching promise starters below, consider your individual responses and then share your thoughts with your co-teacher.

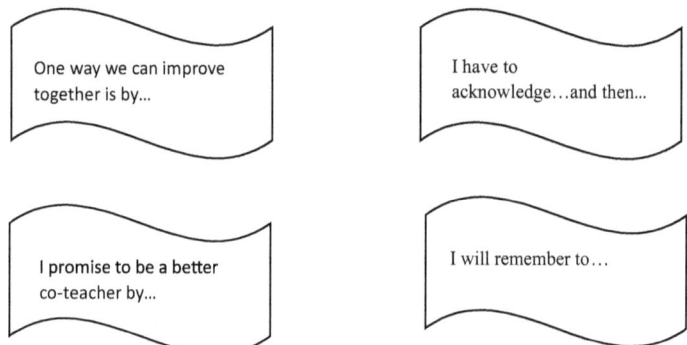

FIGURE 11.1 Co-teaching Promise Starters

Book Discussion Questions

1. Which scenario resonates with you and why? How is this scenario like or unlike an experience you had?
2. Explain why it is so important for co-teachers to be very aware of the specific evidence of how their relationship influences the instructional process and overall learning environment?
3. Select one scenario in this chapter. What advice would you give to the co-teachers in the example? Be specific.

Next Steps in Creating YOUR Co-teaching Power Zone Experiences

An embedded aspect of experiencing co-teaching within the power zone is the role that each co-teacher plays in being an active listener. All of the ideas and activities throughout this book include the skill of active listening as a key component within all aspects of cultivating a growth-fostering co-teaching relationship. Let's review some of the key skills for deeper consideration.

Co-active Listening

Active listening is a strong part of co-teaching in the zone. Co-active listening requires each co-teacher to be deeply attentive and engaged with what their teaching partner is expressing. The aim of co-active listening is for each co-teacher to genuinely understand their teaching partner's perspective—whether they agree or not—and then communicate their understanding back to confirm and reaffirm mutual respect and understanding.

The many activities throughout this book naturally lead you and your co-teacher to be co-active listeners together may you co-create co-active listening, so it remains a solid foundational aspect of experiencing co-teaching in the power zone? All of the activities in this book naturally embed the ways you exercise your co-active listening process. In general, the following steps will lead you and your co-teacher to sustain a co-active listening partnership

1. **Know your co-teacher and the aim of your partnership.** What is your shared vision?
2. **Be self-aware of your own thoughts and actions.** How are your actions working toward your shared co-teaching

vision with your teaching partner? What are your words and actions communicating?

3. **Be mindful of how you are experiencing your co-teacher's words and actions.** How are you interpreting your co-teacher's actions? How are you each impacting the co-teaching experience for and with one another?

The following four listening skills may guide your co-listening process to further optimize your co-teaching experience.

Skill and purpose	How do apply the skill	Example of active listening
Clarify Provides the opportunity for co-teachers to deepen accurate intentions and understanding	Invite your co-teacher to explain some aspect of what they did or said	Let me make sure I understand what you mean... It seems to me that you are... After you (said or did) ....I believe you intended for.... Can you please explain what you meant when you (said...or did...)...?
Paraphrase Provides opportunity to ensure accurate perceptions and clear communication between co-teachers.	Restate what your co-teacher said using your own words or your interpretation of their action(s) to transparently work toward a shared, accurate understanding.	What I am hearing is... From your actions (be specific), it seems you are feeling... It sounds like what's most important to you is...
Reflect Deepens understanding and reveals a level of care, so your co-teacher feels you are working to understand what they are expressing.	Expressing your interpretation for what was said to show you understand your co-teacher's perspective.	I get a sense that you are eager to apply... in class. It sounds to me that you are frustrated with the way things are going because... It seems like you were upset/worried/ confused when...

(*Continued*)

Skill and purpose	How do apply the skill	Example of active listening
Summarize Provides the opportunity for both co-teachers to identify what is most important to the speaker, so they may move forward in harmony even if they have different views.	Blend and integrate ideas and feelings into a clear message to express the key thoughts the speaker is expressing.	Let me summarize what I heard so far. . .. I think I've heard several things that seem to be important to you, first____, second, second____, third____." "It sounds like there are two things that really matter most to you...

When each teacher makes a mindful choice to actively listen to their teaching partner, they forge a commitment to seeing beyond their own perspective. Co-active listening within the CPZ creates a mutually beneficial process that sustains reciprocal, transparent communication throughout all phases of the co-teaching and learning process. Furthermore, the co-active listening process is a natural part of all phases and activities within the CPZ.

Co-teaching Action Step: Puzzle Piece Earned: Reflect: Power of Partnership

Earn your Reflect jigsaw puzzle piece with a focus on how your reflective practices serve to empower you and your co-teaching partner.

Activity: The Power of Partnership

As you continue to reflect on the ideas shared in this book, first take a deep breath, and acknowledge your personal experience in considering co-teaching in the power zone. The questions in the next section will organically guide your personal next co-teaching actions and interactions.

Reflect with the Power of Partnership

- What did you learn about yourself as you consider your role as a co-teacher?
- What did you learn about your co-teacher?
- How is one way you would like to improve?
- What is one way your co-teacher would like to improve?
- How may you support one another?
- Looking at each puzzle piece earned throughout your interactive reading process, what is your own personal strength as a co-teacher? What is your co-teacher's personal strength?

Congratulations! You did it! You earned all the puzzle pieces. You are more than just two puzzle pieces that fit perfectly together! You are a thoughtful, active, empowering educator who is teaching and learning within the co-teaching power zone.

This is only the beginning! Now that you completed this interactive learning about CPZ, what resonates with you moving forward? How may you apply effective actions for all future co-teaching experiences?

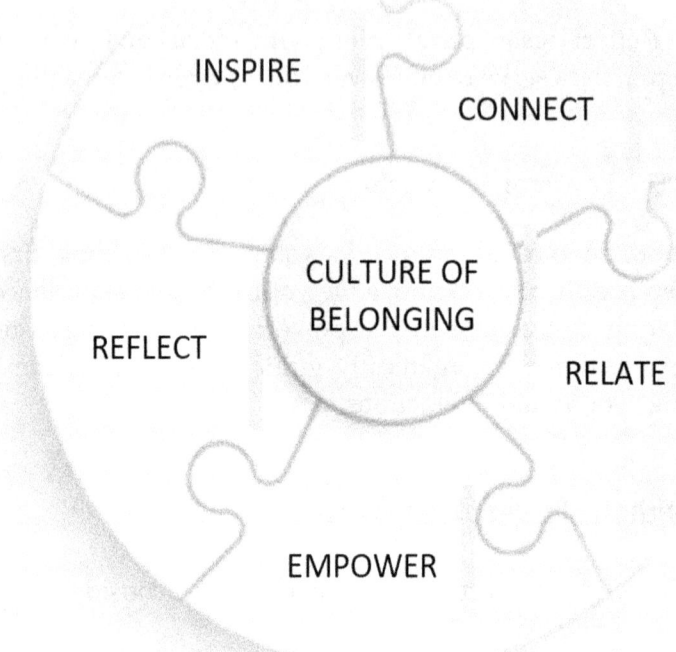

Copyright material from Elizabeth Stein (2024), The Co-Teaching Power Zone, Routledge

References

Allen, K. A., Gray, D. L., Baumeister, R. F., & Leary, M. R. (2022). The need to belong: A deep dive into the origins, implications, and future of a foundational construct. *Educational Psychology Review, 34*(2), 1133–1156.

Anderson, L. W., & Krathwohl, D. R. (2001). *A taxonomy for learning, teaching, and assessing: A revision of Bloom's taxonomy of educational objectives: complete edition*. Longman.

Baumeister, R. F., & Leary, M. R. (1995). The need to belong: Desire for interpersonal attachments as a fundamental human motivation. *Psychological Bulletin, 117*(3), 497.

Bibi, W., Butt, M. N., & Reba, A. (2020). Relating teachers' questioning techniques with students' learning within the context of Bloom's taxonomy. *FWU Journal of Social Sciences, 14*(1), 111–119.

Bondi, S., Daher, T., Holland, A., Smith, A. R., & Dam, S. (2016). Learning through personal connections: Cogenerative dialogues in synchronous virtual spaces. *Teaching in Higher Education, 21*(3), 301–312.

CAST. (2018). *Universal design for learning guidelines version 2.2 [graphic organizer]*. Wakefield, MA: Author.

Cochran, K. F., DeRuiter, J. A., & King, R. A. (1993). Pedagogical content knowing: An integrative model for teacher preparation. *Journal of teacher Education, 44*(4), 263–272.

Cook, L., & Friend, M. (1993). *Educational leadership for teacher collaboration*. https://files.eric.ed.gov/fulltext/ED372540.pdf

Cook, L., & Friend, M. (1995). Co-teaching: Guidelines for creating effective practices. *Focus on Exceptional Children, 28*(3), 1–16.

Deci, E. L., & Ryan, R. M. (2000). The "what" and "why" of goal pursuits: Human needs and the self-determination of behavior. *Psychological Inquiry, 11*(4), 227–268.

Deci, E.L., Ryan, R.M., (1985). Conceptualizations of instrinsic motivation and self-determination. In *Intrinsic and Self-determinatmotivation in human behavior* (pp. 11–14). Plenum Press.

Dove, M. G., & Honigsfeld, A. (2017). *Co-teaching for English learners: A guide to collaborative planning, instruction, assessment, and reflection.* Corwin Press.

Elmesky, R., & Tobin, K. (2005). Expanding our understandings of urban science education by expanding the roles of students as researchers. *Journal of Research in Science Teaching, 42*(7), 807–828.

Emdin, C. (2010). Affiliation and alienation: Hip-hop, rap, and urban science education. *Journal of Curriculum Studies, 42*(1), 1–25.

Fairclough, N. (2015). *Language and power.* Routledge.

Foucault, M. (1982). The subject and power. *Critical Inquiry, 8*(4), 777–795.

Freire, P. (1970). *Pedagogy of the oppressed* (MB Ramos, Trans.). Continuum, 2007.

Freire, P. (2018). *Teachers as cultural workers: Letters to those who dare teach.* Routledge.

Friend, M. (2016). Co-teaching as a special education service: Is classroom collaboration a sustainable practice? *Educational Practice and Reform, 2,* 1–12.

Friend, M & Bursuck, W.D. (2012). Including students with special needs: A practical guide for classroom teachers 6th ed. Pearson.

Friend, M., & Bursuck, W. D. (2002). *Including students with special needs: A practical guide for classroom teachers.* Allyn & Bacon.

Friend, M., & Cook, L. (1992). *Interactions: Collaboration skills for school professionals.* Longman Publishing.

Friend, M., & Reising, M. (1993). Co-teaching: An overview of the past, a glimpse at the present, and considerations for the future. *Preventing School Failure, 37*(4), 6–10.

Friend, M., & Cook, L. (2003). *Interactions: Collaboration skills for school professionals* (4th ed.). Allyn and Bacon.

Friend, M., & Cook, L. (2007). Co-teaching. *Educational Leadership, 64*(5), 48–52.

Friend, M., & Cook, L. (2017). *Interactions: Collaboration skills for school professionals* (8th ed.). Pearson.

Gee, J. P. (2005). The new literacy studies: From'socially situated'to the work. *Situated literacies: Reading and writing in context, 2,* 177–194.

Gee, J. P. (2014). *An introduction to discourse analysis: Theory and method.* Routledge.

Goodenow, C., & Grady, K. E. (1993). The relationship of school belonging and friends' values to academic motivation among urban adolescent students. *The Journal of Experimental Education, 62*(1), 60–71.

Hawkins, D. R. (2014). *Power vs. force.* Hay House, Inc.

Hess, K. (2006). "Applying Webb's Depth-of-Knowledge (DOK) Levels in science." [online] available: http://www.nciea.org/publications/DOKscience_KH08.pdf.

Honigsfeld, A., & Dove, M. (2008). Co-teaching in the ESL classroom. *Delta Kappa Gamma Bulletin, 74*(2), 8.

Johnson, D., & Johnson, R. (1998). Cooperative learning and social interdependence theory. In *Theory and research on small groups* (pp. 9–35). Boston, MA: Springer US. https://www.library.uc.edu.kh/userfiles/pdf/71.Theory%20and%20research%20on%20small%20groups.pdf#page=32

Krathwohl, D. R. (2002). A revision of Bloom's taxonomy: An overview. *Theory into practice, 41*(4), 212–218.

Maslow, A. H. (2013). *Toward a psychology of being.* Simon and Schuster.

McDuffie, K. A., Mastropieri, M. A., & Scruggs, T. E. (2009). Differential effects of peer tutoring in co-taught and non-co-taught classes: Results for content learning and student-teacher interactions. *Exceptional Children, 75*(4), 493–510.

Meyer, A., Rose, D. H., & Gordon, D. (2014). *Universal design for learning: Theory and practice.* CAST Professional Publishing.

Miller, J. B. (1976). *Toward a new psychology of women.* Beacon Press.

Murawski, W. W., & Spencer, S. (2011). *Collaborate, communicate, and differentiate!: How to increase student learning in today's diverse schools.* Corwin Press.

Pugach, M. C., & Winn, J. A. (2011). Research on co-teaching and teaming. *Journal of Special Education Leadership, 24*(1), 36–46.

Rose, D. H., & Meyer, A. (2002). *Teaching every student in the digital age: Universal design for learning.* ASCD.

Roth, W. M., Tobin, K., Zimmermann, A., Bryant, N., & Davis, C. (2002). Lessons on and from the dihybrid cross: An activity–theoretical study of learning in coteaching. *Journal of Research in Science Teaching: The Official Journal of the National Association for Research in Science Teaching, 39*(3), 253–282.

Ryan, R. M., & Deci, E. L. (2017). *Self-determination theory: Basic psychological needs in motivation, development, and wellness.* Guilford Publications.

Sandholtz, J. (2000). Interdisciplinary team teaching as a form of professional development. *Teacher Education Quarterly, 27*(3), 39–54.

Scruggs, T. E., Mastropieri, M. A., & McDuffie, K. A. (2007). Co-teaching in inclusive classrooms: A metasynthesis of qualitative research. *Exceptional Children, 73*(4), 392–416.

Sewell Jr, W. H., & Sewell, W. H. (2005). *Logics of history: Social theory and social transformation.* University of Chicago Press.

Shulman, L. (1987). Knowledge and teaching: Foundations of the new reform. *Harvard Educational Review, 57*(1), 1–23.

Slaten, C. D., Ferguson, J. K., Allen, K. A., Brodrick, D. V., & Waters, L. (2016). School belonging: A review of the history, current trends, and future directions. *The Educational and Developmental Psychologist, 33*(1), 1–15.

Song, W. (2019). Study on the influence of teachers' questioning in high school English reading class on students' critical thinking. *Theory and Practice in Language Studies, 9*(4), 424–428.

Stein, E. (2016). *Elevating co-teaching through UDL.* Cast Professional Publishing.

Stein, E. (2017). *Two teachers in the room: Strategies for co-teaching success.* Routledge.

Stein, E. (2021). *Co-creating a culture of belonging through the relational co-teaching framework: A critical, transformative auto| ethnography* (Doctoral dissertation, Molloy College).

Stein, E. (2023). *Elevating co-teaching with universal design for learning.* CAST Professional Publishing.

Tobin, K. (2006). Learning to teach through coteaching and cogenerative dialogue. *Teaching Education, 17*(2), 133–142.

Tobin, K., & Roth, W. M. (2005). Implementing coteaching and cogenerative dialoguing in urban science education. *School Science and Mathematics, 105*(6), 313–322.

Webb, N. L. (1997). Criteria for alignment of expectations and assessments in mathematics and science education (Council of Chief State School Officers and National Institute for Science Education Research Monograph No. 6). Madison: University of Wisconsin, Wisconsin Center for Education Research.

For Product Safety Concerns and Information please contact our EU
representative GPSR@taylorandfrancis.com
Taylor & Francis Verlag GmbH, Kaufingerstraße 24, 80331 München, Germany

www.ingramcontent.com/pod-product-compliance
Lightning Source LLC
Chambersburg PA
CBHW050552300426
44112CB00013B/1882